Montana Frontier Lawyer

A MEMOIR

LEW L. CALLAWAY

FROM LAW SCHOOL TO CHIEF JUSTICE
AMID PIONEERS & PROSPECTORS
COWBOYS & INDIANS, RUSTLERS & OUTLAWS
1891–1951

INTRODUCTION BY L. L. CALLAWAY, JR.

EDITED BY VIVIAN A. PALADIN

WITH AN APPRECIATION OF CHIEF JUSTICE CALLAWAY'S LEGAL OPINIONS BY ROBERT E. SULLIVAN

Published by Lew L. Callaway, Jr.
in cooperation with SkyHouse Publishers, an imprint of
Falcon Press Publishing Company, Inc., Helena, Montana

Distributed by Falcon Press Publishing Company, Inc.
P.O. Box 1718, Helena, MT 59624
or call 1-800-582-2665

Manufactured in the United States of America

First Edition

Library of Congress Catalog Card Number 91-92236

ISBN 1-56044-076-7

Typeset in Bookman by Desktop Type, Helena, Montana

To Judge Llewellyn L. Callaway and his wife Ellen Badger Callaway and their children, Mimi, Jim, Fan, L.L.C., Jr., and Mary Elizabeth

AN INTRODUCTION TO THE AUTHOR

BY L. L. CALLAWAY, JR.

My father wrote this book more than fifty years ago. It's full of adventures, both in courtrooms and in the Montana wilderness. It's full of people—brave, hard-working, good and honest people—and con men, gold thieves and murderers. Lots of love and laughter and good fellowship are in these stories of the West when it was very young.

The story begins as Lew Callaway, fresh from the University of Michigan Law School, starts his legal career in the little town of White Sulphur Springs, Montana, population 670. His total capital is fifty cents. He has one suit of clothes, two pairs of detachable cuffs, and four collars. The soles of his shoes are so thin he can feel the nails in the wooden sidewalks. He is on his way to fame, if never much fortune. Soon young Callaway is winning his first election, as County Attorney of Madison County, and with it the financial means, $100 per month, to marry his first and only love, beautiful Ellen "Nell" Badger, who was just eighteen.

He was twenty-six, the year was 1894, and from then on he won every election he entered, until 1934. That was the final year of the Great Depression, when he and his fellow Republicans across the country were defeated, almost without exception. That defeat ended his twelve-year career as Chief Justice of the Montana Supreme Court, the highest elective office he ever sought.

My father loved the competition and combat of the courtroom. At the peak of his powers, he may well have been the best trial lawyer in Montana. He rarely lost a case. He understood the law and its reason for being. He particularly liked being a judge. He was fair, impartial, his integrity was unquestioned. James Rowe, a distinguished Montanan who became an advisor to four Presidents (all Democrats), said he was the best Chief Justice in the history of Montana. In his personal life, my father liked almost everyone and everyone who knew him liked and respected him. He was generous, compassionate and warm-hearted. In Montana, he was always with friends, for he had them in abundance in every town and city in the State.

Among his passions was Masonry. He became a Mason at age 21 and it was his consuming interest all his life. He was an active 33rd degree Mason and held the highest Masonic position in the State. His friends jokingly referred to him as "the protestant pope of Montana."

He loved the outdoors and was a legendary hunter and fisherman. He tied his own flies and loaded his own shotgun shells. Frank Linderman, famous for his life among the Indians and his books about them, said of my father, "Lew Callaway always saw more in a tree than a 2x4."

The Judge was a prodigious worker. He wrote for hours every week-end and often in between, mainly on Montana's early history. Fortunately for us, he also wrote about his own life and times, glimpses of which have been compiled in this book.

It seems fitting to me that there be appended to my father's stories an informed appreciation of some of his most important legal decisions on water rights and mining. Happily, the man who consented to undertake this important assignment is the Honorable Robert E. Sullivan of Missoula, a long-time and distinguished friend of my father's.

The reader will soon perceive that Dean Sullivan's "Appreciation" of what he calls the Callaway Court is much more than a dull dissertation about legal matters, without meaning to many of us unless we are lawyers. Instead, calling upon his own vast knowledge and experience, Bob Sullivan asked for and received excellent contributions from other distinguished men in Montana, all of them highly respected and experienced lawyers and educators. The result has much in common with the rest of the book. It informs but is never dull. And like my father's memoirs, it contains many other fascinating elements, including some rare insights into Montana history.

CONTENTS

1

THE EARLY YEARS

The Callaways Arrive in Virginia City

Our First Home

Montana's Capital City in 1871

The Family Settles In

Building a New Home

On a bright, sunny day in March, 1871, Colonel James E. Callaway, accompanied by his wife, Mary Elizabeth, and their son, "Lewie," arrived in Virginia City, Montana Territory. Almost exactly seven years before, President Abraham Lincoln had signed the instrument creating this vast, farflung Western Territory, carved from portions of Idaho and Washington Territories.

Now James Callaway, aged thirty-six, was arriving to become Territorial Secretary (next in succession to Territorial Governor Benjamin Potts). Callaway was appointed by President U. S. Grant, the Army General who had been able, at last, to win the Civil War for the Union and for his Commander-in-Chief, the martyred Abraham Lincoln. There were personal and professional reasons why President Grant had chosen Callaway for this high post in Montana Territory. At the start of the War, Grant had been appointed Colonel of the Twenty-first Illinois Volunteer Regiment, and Captain Callaway had been his adjutant.

Mary Elizabeth Link Callaway was the Colonel's wife, and I was Lewie, their three-year old son. My mother was a handsome, golden-haired woman of twenty-eight, and I, their first child, born December 15, 1868, bore the rather formidable name of Llewellyn Link Callaway. Although of course I don't remember much about the long journey to our new home in Montana, I learned soon enough the details, many of them amusing and all of them of great historical interest. Let me share them now after many years.

Naturally, the travelers were weary. We had come by train from our former home in Tuscola, Illinois, to the end of line at Corinne, Utah. From there we journeyed by Concord stagecoach to Virginia City. It had taken four days and nights of continuous travel in the coach, rumbling and bouncing along at some six miles an hour. Part of the way we were guarded by a detachment of U. S. Cavalry against possible Indian attack!

Before starting to Montana Territory, Secretary Callaway had heard of the awful winters in the Rocky Mountains. Concerned about the safety of his wife and child, he had written to Territorial officials to learn whether it would be safe to bring us out before summer. Since Montana was enjoying a mild winter, the officials had written the new Secretary that they thought he might bring his family without apprehension.

When the telegraph line from Corinne to Virginia City carried the news that the Callaways were coming, the wags in Virginia City got busy. They hunted up all the straw hats and linen dusters they could find. As the stagecoach drew up at the hotel on this lovely warm day in March, they stepped forward clad in this summer attire and inquired solicitously about how Secretary Callaway's wife and child had withstood the rigors of Montana's climate. The Colonel, I later learned, had invited them to the bar.

OUR FIRST HOME

The Callaways were fortunate to find a fine new house for our first home in Virginia City. It was known as the "Rockefellow House." This house still stands today. It was completely restored by Senator and Mrs. Charles Bovey, including the Victorian furniture. A well-built frame house with a lovely view of the surrounding mountains and fairly close to the main part of the little town, it had a "sitting room" on the main floor, well furnished with mahogany Victorian furniture, including chairs covered in red satin—quite elegant. Also on the main floor was a large master bedroom and a fine large kitchen with the usual efficient iron wood-burning stove. The house had its own well. Upstairs were three more bedrooms. There was no running water in the house, of course, and a privy out back, a three holer, drafty in winter.

MONTANA'S CAPITAL CITY IN 1871

Montana Territory in 1871 had a total population of 21,000, not, of course, including the Indians, who in those early days were frequently on the rampage. Virginia City, which became the capital of the Territory in 1865, boasted a population of 1,000. At the height of the gold rush, which began in May, 1863, there were as many as 12,000 men living and working in the settlements that lined Alder Gulch and the adjoining area. When gold sold for $20.00 an ounce, $90 million in gold was taken from this area, 1863 to 1900. (Editor's note: The best estimate of gold production from Alder Gulch is 2,475,000 ounces through 1959. This would amount to approximately $891 million in 1991 dollars).

All of Alder Gulch, which was fourteen miles in length, was one continuous settlement strung along a single street. The progression of the little towns along the gulch was as follows: just out of the lowlands was Junction, then followed Adobetown, Nevada, Central, Virginia City, Pine Grove, Highland, and Summit.

Virginia City, the second capital of Montana Territory, succeeding Bannack, was known throughout the Northwest as "the social city." A mining and commercial town, it was western with all the earmarks, but it contained a remarkable citizenry. There were scholars, musicians, orators—men and women of various types—among its people. The town had theaters, musical and debating societies, dancing parties of the highest type—and others. There were courts, judges, lawyers, federal officers, schools.

The people were friendly and helpful. Good and bad, they were without veneer, genuinely what they were.

Bluffing did not go. There were animosities, of course, but these seldom led to serious trouble.

THE FAMILY SETTLES IN

My parents and I soon fitted into the life of this small Territorial capital, even though I was still so young. But let me also describe my father as I remember him. He was a slim, handsome, five-foot nine-inch, 145-pounder. He sported a military-type beard and looked like what he had been for four long years, a commander of infantry in one of the fight'n'st of the northern regiments, the Twenty-first Illinois Volunteer Regiment. He was a good horseman, as were most of his contemporaries. By profession he was a lawyer, and a good one. As a parliamentarian, he had no equal in the Territory.

Not long after our arrival, the Colonel bought a riding horse, for this was a horse economy, and a man without a horse was in a bad position in this big wide-open country with few roads and long distances. He also bought a buckboard and a horse to draw it. We soon began to enjoy life in this land that had drawn most of its population from the big discovery of gold just eight years before.

When I was five, "Uncle Harry," the colored man, put me on a horse, which he led around. But I don't remember when I learned to ride. The first I remember about riding was when I *was* riding. I used to ride two miles to the post office at Puller Springs when I was eight years old. I rode old Charley, a big white or light grey "government" horse.

Our family liked Montana, especially Virginia City and the surrounding mountain country. It is high country—Virginia City's altitude is 5,822 feet—and great game country.

Father was, of course, busy with the duties of his office as Secretary of the Territory and Acting Governor when Governor Potts was away, which was often.

He also had a law practice to keep him busy. But he was not too busy to start planning to buy land for a ranch and also to build a house in Virginia City.

BUILDING A NEW HOME

During 1880, my father was erecting in Virginia City what was to become the Old Homestead, built on the site of the first public school building in Montana. It was an eight-room house, counting the large living room divided by folding doors. An "old-fashioned" painter grained the pine to make it look like oak. There was a small basement, called the cellar. The house had an unusual room for the time, a bathroom! But without a toilet. The first toilet I ever saw was in the newly built house of Colonel Woolfolk at Sixth and Rodney in Helena. For our bathroom, the water was heated by a "drum" over an old-style boxwood stove.

It was, of course, necessary to get brick for the chimneys. There had been kilns in Alder Gulch, between Nevada and Adobetown, at the time the courthouse was built, but they had disappeared. So my father bought his brick in Glendale, nearly sixty miles away. He brought hay from the ranch, which he stored in the stable he had built on the lots where he was building the house. Then he sent the hired man with a lumber wagon and four horses to Glendale for the brick. The hired man was a lazy, dilatory fellow, and the bricks cost my father a dollar each when they were laid on the lots in Virginia City. And there were a good many bricks. The house had three chimneys. We burned wood, and well do I know it because I had to saw and split it.

BOYHOOD CHORES

We kept a cow in the stable. It was my job to milk her. Sometimes on school days in the winter, it kept me busy milking the cow twice a day, sawing and splitting the wood, carrying it into the house, and doing other chores.

A notably hard winter came in 1880. We experienced several blizzards. During the first one I had to saw wood in the fierce wind and the following severe cold. Usually a blizzard started with a wind which whipped in every direction, followed by three days of intense cold, the thermometer often going to thirty below. After that first blizzard, I sawed extra wood every night and piled it on the back porch. The next blizzard ate it up.

In the winter we lived in Virginia City, where I went to school. The school year was short. Early in the spring of 1875, we went to the Ruby River Valley place, Jessamine Stock Farm, which the Colonel had purchased. This place was to hold many adventures for me. It was eighteen miles from Virginia City. In the buggy it took us three hours to get there.

2

THE MAKING OF A COWBOY

The Jessamine Stock Ranch

Encounters With Indians

Roundup Time, 1880

The Colonel Versus Rattlesnake Jack

Other Adventures on the Ranch

The ranch that was to have such a large influence on my life was purchased from Dr. Leander W. Frary, and it included a herd of extra good cattle. There were some pure Shorthorns among them. To head up the herd, my father bought Leander, a bull bred in Kentucky of a fashionable strain, the Louain. I got to know Leander, the bull with the ring in his nose, very well. The new ranch was named Jessamine after a county in Kentucky. There was a creek of the same name running through the ranch. According to an article in the *Helena Herald* of July 20, 1876, "Territorial Secretary James E. Callaway, now living in Virginia City, . . . is credited with having one of the finest stock ranches in the territory."

ENCOUNTERS WITH INDIANS

In 1877 we heard that the Nez Perce Indians were on the warpath. I remember my father telling Mother about the disastrous Battle of the Big Hole. He said Captain Logan, Lieutenant Bradley, Lieutenant English and many enlisted men were killed. General Gibbon was seriously wounded. The site of the battle was only 137 miles from Helena.

Conditions were none too good, moreover, on the Bannock Reservation in the winter of 1877–78. The government had not kept its promises, and there was much dissatisfaction among the Indians. There was some violence. Notwithstanding this, Chief Tendoy of the Bannocks was maintaining peace as a tribal policy.

In 1878, however, some Bannocks joined with the renegade Nez Perces and went on the warpath. The marauders had no scruples against killing a white man, but the main object seems to have been thieving, with a special design upon horses. The settlers in Ruby Valley heard they were coming but at first did not apprehend serious trouble. There is no doubt that scouts came through the valley, which was already known to the Bannocks in a general way.

One morning I was sent up Jessamine Creek on my new horse, Charley, to find a cow that had stayed out all night. I went to the head of Jessamine but could not find the cow, and so I returned home. I was delayed for some reason, which was the cause of considerable uneasiness on the part of my parents. As I came toward the ranch, I noticed an Indian wickiup pitched on the brow of the bench. It had not been there that morning. Since I was used to Indians, this did not alarm me, not even the fact that the camp was in a strange place, on a hill above and away from the water. Carelessly I came past the wickiup on a lope, into the bottom and into the ranch.

While I had been away, the Indians had come and made camp. Usually they camped down in the bottom near the willows, where wood and water were close at hand. My father remarked to my mother that the placing of the wickiup was odd, but he was not disturbed.

In a little while a large buck and squaw, seemingly in a truculent mood, came to the ranch. No one had been at the ranch since morning except my parents. The woman walked into the kitchen, boldly demanding food. My mother looked toward my father inquiringly, and he said to set out food. The man sat down on the porch, his feet on the ground, beside my father. He spoke in "pidgin" English. Both were looking across the river while the conversation was going on. Father naturally kept his eye on the Indian.

I should have said that both Indians were blanket-clad. Glancing at the buck, my father saw through a parting of the blanket that he was drawing a large knife from its scabbard. Straightening up as rapidly as he could, my father looked across the river as if he saw something, taking care to avoid alarming the Indian. As soon as he got to an erect position, my father sprang into the house past the Indian woman to his needle gun, which was hanging on the wall. Taking the gun and some cartridges, he went outside and loaded the gun in the Indian's presence. He then called for the squaw to come out. When she did, he had them both at his mercy. He told them to get out of there and to get out quick, and, if they ever came back, he would shoot them. My father thought, reviewing the incident, that if he had not been fortunate enough to see the Indian drawing the knife, he and my mother would have been killed, and a massacre of the settlers in the valley would have ensued.

ROUNDUP TIME, 1880

When I was twelve, I began to ride pretty steadily. I wanted to go with the cowboys. My mother objected because of the danger, but the cowboys said they would look after me and I was allowed to go. We got up early on a muggy morning and had a wretched breakfast. The camp cooks were mad, as usual.

Before the horses were all saddled, the sun came out, and it was a beautiful morning. It was June, and the river was high. There was no bridge, and to get to the west side, we had to swim the horses. One of the cowboys asked me if my horse could swim. I said I didn't know. I know I didn't swim, and throughout my life, I never learned how. The cowboy told me that most horses swam without difficulty, but if my horse failed to swim when we got into the river, to slide off behind—not to the side!—and grab his tail. He said, "With you off his back, he'll swim." I said, "When he goes up the bank, he may kick me." "No he won't," the cowboy said, "the first thing he will do after he gets to land, he'll shake hisself." Charley swam perfectly, and when he got to land he surely "shook hisself." He nearly shook me off and almost loosened my teeth.

We rode until midafternoon, combing the hills for cattle, and found them in considerable numbers. All were driven to the river where they were made to swim. There were many young calves which were swept from their mothers' side by the strong current. But those cowboys swam their horses down the turbulent stream and saved every one of them. It took courage to do it, but they did it just as part of the day's work.

The boys who grew up in the valley were not just good cowboys. The necessities of their time and place compelled them to turn their hands to the everyday tasks of the ranchman. They preferred to ride, of course, but they repaired ditches, irrigated the hay lands, built fences, put up hay, and got timber from the mountains, as the exigencies required.

THE COLONEL VERSUS RATTLESNAKE JACK

On this roundup we went into the Sweetwater Basin and with us went men from the Blacktail who had been riding with us. There had been, and was, no disagreement. In the Basin other riders from the Blacktail joined us, among them a newcomer, who was called Rattlesnake Jack. He was a tall man, muscular, wearing a hat with a rattlesnake skin for a band.

About noon I began to hear discussion over an unbranded yearling, a heifer. The Ruby riders said she came from our side of the divide and belonged to our association, which would sell her at auction at the regular time. The Blacktail riders seemed to be agreeing with Rattlesnake Jack that they would take the heifer with their cattle to the Blacktail.

My father, who was captain of the roundup that day, was appealed to, and he said that according to the rules and agreement between the Ruby and Blacktail stockholders, the heifer belonged to us. Then

Rattlesnake Jack became belligerent. Father got off his horse to tighten the cinch. As he did that, Rattlesnake Jack said something abusive. My father bore the reputation of being unafraid of anybody or anything, and it was known he was a fighter. He said, "I don't know you nor care who you are. If you are hunting trouble, you can have it. Get down off your horse and I will fight you anyway you choose and with any weapon. Now fight or shut up." He seemed to grow into the stature of a large man. Rattlesnake Jack said he wasn't hunting a fight, and that settled the affair. We never saw him again.

OTHER ADVENTURES ON THE RANCH

In 1881, my father and Captain James Williams of Vigilante fame who owned land adjoining the Jessamine, became ranch partners. Captain Williams and his family, which included two boys, Jim and John, lived on the ranch the year around. (Editor's note: For Judge Callaway's story of the Montana Vigilantes, see *Montana's Righteous Hangmen: The Vigilantes in Action*, University of Oklahoma Press, 1981.)

Early in 1882, Captain Williams had received word from the giant Poindexter & Orr ranching partnership that they were planning a big roundup in the Blacktail Valley. Since the Ruby and Blacktail cattle crossed the Sweetwater Divide and intermingled, and since Poindexter & Orr intended to sell a large number of the cattle from their range, Captain Williams knew he had better go over and protect his and my father's interests. So on about the first of May, he concluded to go to the Poindexter & Orr ranch. He took his oldest son, Jim, and me with him.

It was about a thirty mile ride and took practically all day. We took our blankets with us. Arriving and taking off our saddles, we inquired as to where we should turn our horses. The Poindexter & Orr man said, "Turn 'em into the calf pasture." The calf pasture on our ranch at home was a field of, say, ten acres. I asked, "Where is the calf pasture?" and the cowboy said, "Oh, here, anywhere." So I asked, "Where is the next fence?" and he answered, "About ten miles; turn 'em out, we'll get 'em in the morning." We made our beds on the ground. I was fourteen years old, and it was my first big roundup.

We helped punch 6,000 head of cattle up Blacktail to the Red Rock divide. The day was hot, the drive slow. It was necessary to get the mass of cattle strung out for the long drive. First went the steers and young stock. Experienced cowboys took this bunch, which was easy to drive, and about all they had to do was to direct the course and ride along behind gossiping. The next bunch was composed of strong cows, calves, and some young stock. That was easy too, because the cattle were inclined to follow pretty close to the lead bunch.

But the "drag" was different. It was composed of the old cows, cows with young calves, and cattle that were ailing for one reason or another. The drag walked through a cloud of dust. Some of the cattle tried to break away; the bunch was unruly. Of course they would put the old men and boys on the drag. One could hardly breathe. I concluded to get out of it. A yearling dodged out of a bunch, and I took after her immediately. I chased her into the second bunch. The first chance I got, I scared a yearling out of that bunch and eased it to the lead. I stayed there for the duration of the drive.

I know I was at the ranch in 1883. Worse than that: my father and Captain Williams conceived the idea of digging a long ditch from the river to cover the Jack Creek bench. Charley Mead, a civil engineer, was employed and set to work. I was rodman. By the method employed, we had to drive a stake every chain, sixty-five feet. That duty fell to me. So we had to make the stakes every night. We took our lunch with us every day. It was a long, hard job. We actually surveyed over thirteen miles of ditch that was never dug. The expense was prohibitive. Then came haying. There was much pleasure in this, despite the hard work.

I went to the ranch on March 24, 1884, and it was the best year of my boyhood. Jim and John Williams were eager to see me, and I was in the same frame of mind towards them. I doubt if three boys were ever more congenial. We went into the saddle at once and did little else but ride until haying time, which was about August 1 that year.

I went back East to school in December, 1884, and did not return until 1886.

3

EASTERN EDUCATION OF A YOUNG COWBOY

To Philadelphia and Prep School
A Montana Cowboy Fights Back
University Studies Begin
Death of Captain James Williams
Back to the Ranch
A Return to Ann Arbor
Becoming a Mason and a Lawyer

My mother and father had been discussing my future education. It was taken for granted that I would have the privilege of a college education. They hoped that I would become a lawyer. They also realized that the schooling I had been getting in Virginia City would not be adequate preparation for college. Therefore it was decided I would go to preparatory school in Philadelphia.

There were two strong reasons for choosing Philadelphia. First, it was well known for its many cultural advantages. It had famous colleges and universities and excellent preparatory schools. It had fine museums and theatres and a great Art Institute. Philadelphia's historical importance as the city where the Declaration of Independence was written and promulgated made it dear to the heart of every American.

Second, the Callaways had relatives living in Philadelphia so that I would have the advantages of a home away from home while I was attending school. The savings from this arrangement would also be substantial. Samuel Daggy, "Uncle Daggy" and his wife Aunt Sue, my mother's aunt, her mother's sister, lived at 4004 Chestnut Street in one of the best parts of Philadelphia.

So in December, 1884, my journey towards getting an education began. The stagecoach left Virginia City at 8:00 A.M. My father gave me $250.00 to make the trip. He told me to stop in Chicago and go from there to Tuscola, Illinois, where we had relatives, and from there to continue my journey to Philadelphia. My father rode down as far as Central and left me with some emotion. I had fuzz on my face from the day before. At my father's suggestion, I had gone to the barber shop and got a shave. I thought I was quite a man. I was sixteen years old.

I bought a berth on the Pullman at Dillon and I thought it was a palatial affair. But I was thrifty. I rode in the day coach by day, taking a Pullman by night.

I spent Christmas and New Year's in Tuscola with my relatives and then took a train for Indianapolis. Eventually I arrived in Philadelphia. It was, I think, January 3, 1885. I went out in front of the Broad Street Station and beheld wonderland, the great public buildings of Philadelphia. The marble was white, gleaming in the morning sunlight. The buildings were enormous. It was one of those lasting impressions.

I said to a cabby, "I want to go to 4004 Chestnut Street." He said, "Is that the same as forty-hundred and four?" I told him it was, and we set out. It was about three miles and very cold. The humidity made it worse to me.

At 4004, I met Uncle Daggy and Aunt Sue. Aunt Sue was as fine a woman as ever lived and Uncle Daggy was a fine man. They rented their house in this fashionable neighborhood from a high-toned young doctor named Guy Hinsdale for his keep. This doctor knew "all the answers" when it came to conventions. He taught me what to do. He soon saw that I was ignorant. When he and I were walking together and he tipped his hat, a derby, to a lady acquaintance, I was to do the same thing. I never heard of such a custom. He taught me many other things that he knew and I had never heard of. We got to be very good friends. I suppose it was the next morning after I arrived that Uncle Daggy took me to the West Philadelphia Academy, or "West Rugby," where I was to attend school.

MONTANA COWBOY FIGHTS BACK

This was a high-toned school attended by boys from wealthy families. They were all rich but me. It was a tough assignment for me. The other boys had entered in September and were all acquainted. They called me "country" right off. They heard I was from Montana, but unknown to me, there was a town in western Pennsylvania called Montana, and they supposed I was from there.

I guess I was country enough and deserved the name, but when they found I was from the Rocky Mountains, the Far West, it was different. They wanted to know all about Indians and cowboys and bears. They annoyed, embarrassed me. I didn't think there was anything strange about Indians or cowboys or bears. Had I only known it, I could have told them yarns by the hour, some with the exercise of a little imagination to make their hair stand on end.

After the newness of the boy from the Far West wore off, they started to ride me. Two of them were particularly offensive. One morning, after I had grown pretty tired of it, something happened. These two boys were both larger than I, but I was hard as nails and exceptionally strong for my size. I don't remember what it was that started the row, but I jammed one of them through a glass door and dragged him downstairs, which used him up pretty thoroughly. Turning upon the other one who had come along to help his fellow, I literally wiped up the basement floor with him. I suppose I ruined his suit besides nearly scaring him to death. They found out something of the Wild West. There was an investigation over the affray, but nothing came of it. The headmaster told me to keep my mouth shut; so far as he was concerned, he was glad of it.

My one friend in Philadelphia from Virginia City was James P. "Finny" Deimling. He had been sent to the city by his father, Colonel Deimling, early in the 1880s. Finny lived a ways out on Eighth Street. As soon as I could get straightened around, I went to see him and his brother, Will, who had also been sent there sometime before I arrived.

There was, of course, no telephone. I wanted news from home. It was three weeks after I left home before I received a letter. It was 3,000 miles and I knew no one in Philadelphia except the Deimling boys. I couldn't say I knew Uncle Daggy or Aunt Sue, or Dr. Hinsdale, as yet. One can be lonesome on a ranch or out in the mountains, but that's nothing compared to being lonesome in a great city.

Eventually I spent a great deal of time with the Deimlings, especially Will. Nearly every Saturday we were together. We went to Independence Hall, across to Camden by ferry, to the League Island Navy Yard where the wartime monitors were floating in the river, to Fairmont Park, to the Baldwin Locomotive Works, to the Academy of Fine Arts, to this theatre or that, to the cemeteries, to the grave of Benjamin Franklin. We did it all on foot. It wasn't long before we knew more about Philadelphia than boys who were reared there.

My preparatory days in Philadelphia ended after eighteen months, during which time I was told I had compressed three years of work. I was afraid that some of my preparation was faulty, and later found that it was, although I really worked hard.

UNIVERSITY STUDIES BEGIN

From Philadelphia, I went to Ann Arbor, to take entrance exams for admittance to the University of Michigan. In the exams, I got along well in algebra, well enough to pass in plane geometry. I did well in Greek, English, history and geography. I had a condition in Latin. I read Caesar at sight, was satisfactory in Virgil and Sallust, but had not read the six orations of Cicero, and never did read them in Latin.

Thus after all my fears that I was not sufficiently prepared after my time at prep school, I managed to pass the entrance exams to the University of Michigan satisfactorily.

After a hiatus at home, I went back to Ann Arbor in the Fall of 1886, matriculated, and entered the class of 1890, looking to the degree of bachelor of arts. I started in with the intention of having a studious year. I was taking Latin, French, German, calculus, trigonometry, oratory, and perhaps something else.

My Latin was under the instruction of Walter Miller. We were studying Livy. I sat next to Jimmy Angell, the son of the President of the University, who later was President of Yale. Jimmy was good at Latin, knew what the professor wanted. I could read the text, but I had never been stopped and asked to explain the construction of the sentence, decline a noun, nor conjugate a verb. I had supposed I was past that. It bothered me, and I did not do well.

Trigonometry and calculus I hated, and I got no help from the instructor. I was discouraged. I disliked the professor of oratory, detested his way of teaching. It seemed to me that his methods were artificial and mechanical and that the hearer would detect insincerity and embellishment in the speaker's discourse that would obscure the earnestness of the speaker so that his language would fail to persuade. It simply would be a lot of sound, conveying little meaning to the hearer. My idea was that an auditor should listen with a disposition to be convinced. I got mad and quit the course. Whether I was wrong or not, I have seen many a lawsuit lost through supposed oratory and won by honest, unembellished argument. I never had any trouble winning a case before a jury if I had a fair chance with the facts.

Perhaps my main difficulty at the University was that I got to running around too much. There was intense rivalry between the sophomores of '89 and the freshmen of '90. Hazing was in vogue, and I was right in it. The class of 1890 had an unusual number of athletes—boxers, wrestlers, foot racers, and active fellows like myself. We made '89 miserable. They were afraid to show themselves in the street at night. If one ventured forth, we put him over the fence. This was done by catching him by the hands and feet. If he fell on his hands and feet like a cat, all right. Some adventurous sophomores would see a small group of freshmen together and yell "'89 look out!" We caught them and put them over the fence.

For the second semester, I took a lighter schedule. I cannot remember what it was. I know that I attended Professor Thomas's classes. I did this faithfully. From the beginning I did some considerable reading in the library. Among the men who used to come to my room at Mrs. Southmayd's was Moses Gomberg. He liked to talk religion. He told me about Darwin and Huxley, made sport of Genesis, the story of Jonah and the whale, and other Biblical stories. I read Darwin's *The Descent of Man*, and books by Huxley and Kincaid.

DEATH OF CAPTAIN JAMES WILLIAMS

In February, 1887, letters from home told me they were having a terrible winter. The cattle were suffering. The feed was about gone. The range was poor. Captain Williams killed himself on February 21, 1887. He had been drinking some at Puller Spring as conditions grew worse, but not on that day.

He had gone to Virginia City about a week before and talked with Mr. Elling, the banker, about money matters. Elling felt that he could not loan him any more. While in town, Captain Williams bought a bottle of laudanum.

On February 21, he went to the lower field to see the cattle. They were starving, humped up with their heads to the ground. It was snowing. Captain Williams was near a heavy copse of willows. He walked 100 yards toward Puller Springs, then backtracked to the willows, entering some sixty feet into their midst. How he got through the thick willows I don't know. They had to cut a passageway to get his body out. When he got to the end, he lay down, put his mittens under his head, drank the laudanum, and went to sleep.

BACK TO THE RANCH

Letters from home told me of the bad conditions. Along in May 1887, I was told to come home early. Aunt Min and Cousin Lou met me in Chicago and came west with me. We got to Bozeman and took a team to Virginia City. I reached Virginia City the first week in June and went to the ranch.

We needed some more fencing on the ranch. The end of the open range cattle business was at hand. Indeed, it had arrived, although I did not realize it. There was still open range, and we had cattle scattered here and there. But we were engaged in trying to convert a cattle ranch into a farm. A white man got into difficulty with Tom Farrell, who accused him of stealing a meerschaum pipe. My father got the fellow off and received in payment a beautiful chestnut sorrel rideling about four years old. This was a remarkable horse, part thoroughbred. He weighed about 950 pounds, and was about fifteen hands high. His stride in loping was an ordinary fence panel. He was smart, but heady. He wanted to run all the time, and as he was so much faster than the horses in the valley, I had to ride alone. Even then he would work himself into a lather by whirling around in the road, dancing, with a curved neck. He was difficult to mount. When I got my left foot in the stirrup, the finish of the mounting was with the horse in the air. When in the saddle I had to ride every minute. He was not as good a cow horse as Jailbird, my other horse. He was too fast, but I punched cows with him just the same. He was good in running range horses because he could outrun them and loved to do it. But as long as he was a stallion he was a good deal of a nuisance. I hated to do it, but I came to the conclusion that I had to geld him. So one day when Charley Pendarvis, a good cutter, came along, I had the situation remedied. After that the horse, named by me Firefly, was somewhat subdued. He remained a great horse.

A RETURN TO ANN ARBOR

I went back to Ann Arbor in October 1889, a little late for the semester. I felt my poverty and didn't know how I was going to make it even with the $300.00 I was going to borrow from Mr. Conner. I had to go back to Virginia City at Christmas time to go upon my 80 acre timber-culture entry on which I had filed.

Charles O. Knudsen, a classmate with whom I had been slightly acquainted as a junior, also got in late. He hunted me up and wanted to room with me. He had looked at a room out near the new hospital, which he could get cheap, but we would have to saw our own wood. I believe the room was only $1.50 per week.

Because I had gotten to campus late, I had to take examinations at the beginning of the semester, passing all of them. I never took another examination. The law school faculty had the policy of passing a student "on his record" if his average was of a certain grade.

I had gotten over my foolishness. My idea was to learn all I could, to prepare myself to be a lawyer. In fact, I did so well that I obtained permission from the dean to take extra work in the literary department.

The work in the first semester was hard. We had Blackstone, contracts, domestic relations, commercial law, and some other subjects. The lessons in Blackstone were very long, sometimes forty pages. Some of the chapters were tough. Corporeal and incorporeal hereditaments were hard for a beginner.

BECOMING A MASON AND A LAWYER

Along in the Fall, I was walking with George W. Burt, a boy from Illinois. Noticing a Masonic pin on his vest, I asked if he were a Mason. He said yes, and I said I would be twenty-one in December, and I wanted to be a Mason if I could. He said he would be glad to take my petition. Perhaps I would have wanted to join the Masons anyhow. I was inclined that way because of conditions in Virginia City, where most of our best friends among the men wore Masonic pins.

When I turned twenty-one on December 15, I talked with George Burt again and he took in my petition. In due time I was elected, took the first and second degrees in February, and my Master Mason's degree on March 17, 1890. After I had taken my first degree, the very next day, I bought a Masonic pin, poor as I was, and wore it for many years. There were in Ann Arbor many fraternities, but they did not come near me. I was too poor, and not inclined to "mix." They exulted in their pins, some very expensive. I did not envy them. My modest Masonic pin, in enduring satisfactions, was worth all of theirs put together.

It was expected that we would soon receive a list of those who had passed on their records. If we passed, that meant we would be recommended to admission to the bar. The list was posted, and my name was there. Shortly thereafter a number of us received a notice to appear at the courtroom of Judge Kinne, the superior judge, to undergo an examination for admittance to the bar. We had been expecting it, but there was great trepidation. Naturally, some thought they were weak in a particular subject, and they concentrated on that. Many made notations on their cuffs.

The fateful morning arrived, and some two hundred of us appeared in Judge Kinne's courtroom. It was announced that the three-man committee to examine us consisted of Judge Kinne, a prominent Ann Arbor lawyer, and Professor Bradley M. Thompson. Professor Thompson had taught us equity jurisprudence and other subjects, and we liked him. He was a benevolent, fatherly type of man, with a full grey beard.

Judge Kinne announced that the Ann Arbor lawyer had been called to Detroit and hence could not attend the examination. Therefore, he would call in Professor Thompson to proceed. Professor Thompson rose, saying in substance, "If Your Honor please, any examination on my part would be a work supererogation. I have been examining these young gentlemen for about two years, and I can assure Your Honor *that they are all well qualified.*" The words italicized are exactly what he said; I shall never forget them.

Judge Kinne wiggled in his high seat, stern in appearance, and said: "Well, if that's the case, the practical part of the examination falls to me." A chill ran down my backbone. I needed a stimulant. Judge Kinne continued, "All who expect to engage in the practice of law stand and raise their right hands." We did so. "Mr. Clark, administer the oath to these young gentlemen as attorneys, counselors, and solicitors at law." After the oath was administered, the judge smilingly congratulated us upon our admission, saying that he trusted we would discharge our new duties with pleasure, fidelity, and success. Thereupon we rushed forth to celebrate and, incidentally, to get some stimulant, of which we had been sorely in need. I suppose there was an unprecedented consumption of beer in Ann Arbor. A professor moved our admission at Lansing before the Supreme Court of Michigan, which was granted. I never saw the Supreme Court of Michigan in session. Sol Hepner, my classmate, moved my admission in Montana while I was in White Sulphur Springs. The Supreme Court admitted me. I did not sign the roll of attorneys until during my first elective term as Chief Justice.

The big event of the spring was the baseball game featuring Michigan vs. Cornell. Michigan won eight to six. Two train loads of Michigan students went to Detroit to see this game. After the great victory, most of the men managed to get drunk, or close to it. I got back to Ann Arbor at 3:00 A.M. The next morning I was afraid I *wouldn't* die. After my recovery, I was a good boy. I never again went on a college binge, not even when I was admitted to the bar.

Commencement came with its myriads of expectations. Diplomas were handed out. The next day I started home the cheapest way I could go. I slept on the car seats and on benches at the stations. Michigan Central to Chicago, the Milwaukee to St. Paul, the Northern Pacific to Norris, and finally the stage. I got off the stage downtown in Virginia City and walked up the hill to our house. My mother saw me coming, and came to meet me, exclaiming, "Oh Red, Red!" This was because I, like most of the seniors, had grown a full beard, and it was certainly red.

I went to the ranch almost immediately and found much to do. Then came a letter from Attorney Max Waterman asking me to come to White Sulphur Springs. So on July 28, 1891, I set off for my first job, and the beginning of my career in law.

4

BEGINNINGS OF A CAREER

Arrival in White Sulphur Springs
Reporting for Work
Close Encounter With the Badger Family
The Supreme Court and My First Cases

I began practicing law in White Sulphur Springs, Montana, on July 31, 1891. I was not quite 23 years old. There was no vision on my part as to where in Montana Territory I would begin my career; it was determined by Max Waterman, a White Sulphur Springs attorney already mentioned. A Michigan alumnus himself, Waterman had written to the Dean of the Law School saying that he needed someone to assist him in his practice. He asked that the Dean recommend a law student graduating in 1891. In his letter, Waterman described the kind of man he wanted. I think, as a fact, that there was no such excellent man in the graduating class.

The Dean's secretary, however, showed me the letter and said that, since I was from Montana and a good student, the Dean was going to recommend me and that it would be the first recommendation given by the faculty that year. It was suggested that I write to Mr. Waterman, which I did, informing him that I would be home late in June, 1891, and that he could communicate with me if he wished.

In due time I received a letter from Mr. Waterman asking me to come to White Sulphur Springs, so I began making preparations at once. I must have left my parents' home in Virginia City on July 28, because I was on a four-horse stagecoach driven by Will Ennis, leaving Ennis for Norris on the 29th. We reached the town of Townsend at midnight. The stage stopped and I got off; the night was black. A dim light came towards me, and a voice said, "Do you want to go to a hotel?" I said, "Yes, the best one," and the man replied, "That will be damned easy." He took me to the Townsend Hotel, which was as bad as I feared it would be. The signs announced that the stage would leave for "W. S. Springs" at 8:00 A.M., so I left a call for 6:30. The bed was poor, but I was tired and slept soundly.

The next morning the weather was fair and my hopes were high. I was going to fame and fortune! It was forty miles to "W. S. Springs," and the driver, whose name was Tripp, was taciturn. We ambled along not saying a word, over a hot ridge into Deep Creek canyon, following up the Creek for twelve miles to a spot they called the Carpenter place. This was formerly a favorite camping site of traveling Indians. We proceeded up the crooked, picturesque canyon, crossing fifty-two bridges over Deep Creek, and thence to the top of the mountain.

The canyon was beautiful. Deep Creek was clear as crystal and full of trout. Grouse ran across the road, and there were deer in the adjacent hills. From the top of the mountain, it was three or four miles to the Charles W. Cook ranch, and from there across a flat valley it was ten miles to White Sulphur Springs.

The driver told me that the best hotel in town was the Higgins House, and we drove to it. It was a brick building extending nearly half across the main street. I was to learn that Dr. William Parberry had laid out the town, and that James Higgins, his enemy, who owned the adjoining land, laid out an addition and refused to conform to Dr. Parberry's streets. Higgins built the hotel on his own land, of course. I was to learn, too, that it wasn't the best hotel in town; it wasn't run very well either. The very evening I arrived, the cook, in a rage, had intentionally cut some fingers off a waitress with a meat cleaver. If the law took any action about this outrage, I never heard of it.

The next morning, after I paid my bill, I had a fifty cent piece in my pocket. That's all the money I had in the world. I have that fifty cent piece still. I had one suit of clothes, two suits of underwear, two white shirts, two pairs of detached cuffs, four collars. The soles of my shoes were so thin that the nails in the wooden sidewalks of White Sulphur Springs hurt my feet.

On reporting in to Max Waterman at his law office, I found out that my new employer did not like the man who ran the Higgins House, and recommended that I go to the White Sulphur Springs Hotel operated by one Max Sklower. Mr. Waterman also guaranteed the price of two comforters and a pillow which I purchased, and arranged for a room with a bedstead and springs on it in a suite occupied by Charley Wight and Dr. Thomas Antisell. Mr. Wight was County Clerk of Meagher County, and very helpful. He and I became firm friends. I was also friendly with Dr. Antisell. We could not see then what fate had in store for him.

> "Heaven from all creatures hides the book of fate,
> All but the page prescribed, their present state."

Dr. Antisell was a well educated, studious man, quiet in demeanor. I saw nothing unusual about him. It was a shock when melancholia seemed to possess him; it grew steadily worse and he passed from my sight forever. When I saw him last he was on his way to the State Hospital.

REPORTING FOR WORK

In the beginning, precisely on July 31, 1891, Mr. Waterman put me to work at probate and collection work, and briefing. There was a large amount of mining litigation in the office but not a single case was briefed. I familiarized myself with the decisions in the Montana Reports and in Morrison's Mining Reports. I could give from memory the book and page of every mining case in Montana. I knew many United States Supreme Court cases the same way. The mining litigation in the office arose mostly over locations, discovery, marking boundaries, recording. Waterman's practice was a very general one, containing most everything one encounters in this western country.

I had not made any close friends as yet, and put in my time at night studying in the office. Coming out of

Law School, I thought I knew some law, but I had a rude awakening. I read, time and again, the chapters of Greenleaf on competent, material and relevant evidence. The result was that I was soon equipped with a working knowledge of evidence, perhaps better than most lawyers my age. That knowledge, in fact, has served me throughout my well-nigh fifty years of experience on the floor and on the bench.

It was good that I was forced to learn quickly, for Mr. Waterman soon went away somewhere, leaving me alone in the office. He had no more than left town when Irvin Smith, a local blacksmith, and a client of the office, came in to see Mr. Waterman. A tall, elderly colored man, Mr. Smith indeed had a tale of woe to tell. It seems he had loaned a man some money, taking as security a six-horse team and two wagons, for which the man had given him a chattel mortgage. But now, Smith told me, the man had gathered up his goods, loaded them in the wagons, hitched up his horses, and was preparing to leave the country. Brer Smith wanted his debtor stopped.

I told the old man I would do something right away. But I didn't know just what. An injunction would do the job, I felt sure. It occurred to me that I would need a copy of the chattel mortgage anyhow, so I went to the office of the County Clerk and told Charley Wight what I wanted, and why. My obliging friend gave me a certified copy, saying, "You will find a good direction to the Sheriff in the case of Maddox v. Rader. It's in the last Montana Report which has just come in. There's a copy of the Report in Badger's office."

CLOSE ENCOUNTER WITH THE BADGER FAMILY

Mr. Badger was the Clerk of the Court, whom I had met a day or two before. So I went to his office, and Woodson, Badger's son who was also acting as his deputy, gave me the Ninth Montana Report. The case told me exactly what to do. I made the proper endorsement on the chattel mortgage, which I then gave to Sheriff Rader, who soon overhauled the escaping mortgager with the property.

While this was going on, someone came into the office wanting a chattel mortgage drawn. I drew it and charged the man $3.00, which he paid. I then borrowed a pair of shoes from Charley Wight, but they were too large, so I stuffed some paper in the toes. I wore these until I could get my own shoes half-soled. Little did I know that meeting Mr. Badger and his son, Woodson, was infinitely more important in my life than learning how to draw up and execute a chattel mortgage, or even having funds at last to have my shoes half-soled.

Meanwhile, I had another rude awakening: I had a large number of ready-made enemies. Waterman's enemies were mine, and he had plenty of them. I had made inquiries concerning my employer before coming to White Sulphur Springs, and the information I got was favorable. After going into his office, however, I found people who said Waterman wouldn't pay his debts, he wasn't straight, he was crooked in his practice, and so on. And of course, by their lights, I was the same kind of man. I had some disagreeable experiences on this account. To make matters worse, I was shy, diffident and bashful, so I had to put on a "front," which caused people to accuse me of being conceited. I was anything but that!

THE SUPREME COURT AND MY FIRST CASES

In spite of these difficulties, I went ahead, striving to do good work. I tried and won my first case before the Montana Supreme Court in January 1892, less than six months from the time I arrived in White Sulphur Springs (Milot v. Reed, 11th Montana Report). Inside a year, I appeared in the Supreme Court three times. And gradually I made some friends.

My first case was defending Patsy Jefferson, a

cowboy, who was charged with stealing a six-shooter. The jury found him not guilty.

In a short time, Mr. Waterman sent me to Castle, a mining camp located about twenty-five miles away over the Castle Mountains, to try a case in the Justice Court. Castle was a typical mining camp, employing about 150 miners, and others who worked in related businesses. There were more saloons than were needed, if a saloon ever is needed, and much gambling. These ran all night. The hotel in which I stayed had a front door opening onto the sidewalk; from the rear of the second story, one stepped out on a hill. There was a pitcher of water sitting in a wash bowl on the washstand, and a slop jar on the floor. The bed was a place on which one might lie down, might sleep.

The lawyer on the other side was one J. M. Addle, and he was the real thing in a Justice Court. He demanded a jury, and despite my best efforts, beat me without difficulty. I came back to White Sulphur crestfallen and discouraged, vowing revenge. The opportunity to get it did not come for about a year, but it did come.

There was a willful girl in Castle named Mary Cordero. She thought her father was influential, and that made her worse. In school she was disobedient and obstreperous; also husky. These qualities got her into trouble with her teacher. Attempting to punish Miss Cordero, the teacher, a woman, called on another teacher, also a woman, for help. The two teachers whipped the pupil soundly, whereupon Mr. Cordero swore out a warrant for their arrest.

The school trustees and other sympathizers resolved that the teachers should have the best lawyer in Meagher County, so they sent for Mr. Waterman. He didn't like to travel and sent me. Doubtless Waterman was an overmatch for Counselor Addle. When I arrived, the trustees and other friends of the teachers were much disappointed. One, Mrs. Barnes, a great friend of the Badger family, was one of those pious people who have neither tact nor human sympathy. She told me, a youngster who needed encouragement, that they wanted Mr. Waterman and they were greatly disappointed that I had come in his stead. Naturally, this did little for my morale.

Undaunted, I bought two good cigars and called on the Justice. While we smoked, I encouraged him to talk over the old days, and we discussed a number of other topics. We did not talk about the upcoming case, although I did tell him I would "appear tomorrow for the defense." Addle was purporting to represent the State. The County Attorney, Napoleon B. Smith, perhaps did not know anything about it.

Court convened. I entered a plea of not guilty on behalf of the defendants, and waived a jury trial. Then Addle went into action. He said that I could not cut off the State's right to a jury. I challenged his right to speak for the County Attorney. This flabbergasted him. We argued the points at length, Addle showing much heat. The Justice sustained me.

Addle jumped up, shouting his dismissal of the case. I moved that the costs be assessed against the complaining witness, Cordero. The Justice sustained the motion. Addle and Cordero stamped out.

The trustees, teachers and their friends were profuse with compliments, which abashed me somewhat. As we were beginning to disperse, a man came running up the steps and into the Courtroom. He urged me to go down the back steps because Addle was drinking and threatening to beat me within an inch of my life. Others told me to avoid Addle, who was a man six feet tall and strongly built. I said no, I would not run from him. A number of friends walked down the street with me.

As we passed a saloon, I saw Addle at the bar, and he saw me. Fearing he might think it was a retreat on my part if I kept on going, I walked into the saloon and said, "Now, Addle, didn't I give you a good licking?" He replied, "You bet you did, have a drink!" I said I would take a cigar and we parted as friends. The school trustees asked me whether Addle could start the case again; I said probably, but I didn't think he would. They said, "If he does, come yourself; don't send Waterman!"

Finally feeling as though I had "arrived" as a full-fledged lawyer, I went back to White Sulphur Springs ready to practice law and enjoy a full personal life as well.

5

THE LAW & ADVENTURE IN WHITE SULPHUR SPRINGS

The Cumberland Mining Case

A Near Miss With Frozen Feet

Given Up For Dead

My Friend Austin Gormley

Correcting a Miscarriage of Justice

In September, 1891, Mr. Waterman became excercised over the impending trial of Riggs v. the Cumberland Mining Company. Court was shortly to convene. The contest was over a conflict between a mining claim owned by Riggs and the Cumberland No. 2, located by the Cumberland Mining Company. The Cumberland itself was the principal claim in Castle. Probably there were 100 miners working in it. It was a huge deposit in lime rock. At the 400-foot level, there had been dug out what the miners referred to as a "room," which was wholly in ore. It must have been 25 or 30 feet in diameter and 20 feet high; the shaft came into it. The ore had been shipped to Livingston, 75 miles away, and smelted there. A geologist would have known that in all probability it was a chute and that the chute did not extend into the Cumberland No. 2; but if it did, that claim was valuable.

There was enough of a vein in the Riggs discovery to sustain a location; it was probably a small chute having no relation to the deposit in the Cumberland.

The plaintiff Riggs was represented by Max Waterman, William Wallace, Jr., and H. G. McIntire. I was law clerk. The Cumberland was represented by N. B. Smith, N. W. McConnell, and T. C. Bach. This was an unusual group of lawyers.

Sketching out the men who represented Riggs, I will start with my employer, Max Waterman, who, as I have already indicated, did not have a spotless personal reputation. But he was nonetheless a good trial lawyer, especially good with witnesses.

William Wallace, Jr. was a very brilliant young attorney, a protege of E. Warren Toole, then and for many years head of the Montana Bar and unsurpassed in the Northwest. Wallace was a student and a prodigious worker. He was fine with witnesses, especially on cross examination. Few men in my observation have talked more effectively to a jury. Summed up, I think Wallace was the best all-around lawyer I ever knew. He later became Division Counsel for the Northern Pacific in Montana, Assistant Attorney General of the United States, and one of the foremost lawyers of New York City.

Henry G. McIntire was exceptionally well educated in the *belles lettres* and the law. He was a profound student and perhaps was technically the best lawyer in Montana. McIntire spoke almost faultless German and had a large German clientele. He had been educated at Freiberg, or maybe it was Heidelberg. But he was a supercilious, sarcastic, and conceited man, which offended many.

On the other side the leading counsel for the Cumberland was Newton W. McConnell, an able and powerful lawyer and an eloquent talker to a jury. McConnell had been a judge in Tennessee and for some time Chief Justice of Montana by appointment by President Grover Cleveland.

Thomas C. Bach had been an Associate Justice of the Supreme Court and was an able lawyer, but not a success with a jury. He was a fastidious man and somewhat resembled McIntire in his mannerisms.

Napoleon B. Smith was a good lawyer, conservative in thought. He had a fine line of clients, and was known for his honesty. While he was not a good speaker, juries trusted him.

The contest was strongly waged on both sides, and I learned a good deal of the practical side of a mining lawsuit. The focal point was whether a discovery had been made by Riggs or by the locators of the Cumberland No. 2.

During the trial, I went to Castle with several practical miners to examine the Cumberland No. 2 discovery. Was there a well-defined wall? They claimed one wall only. The shaft was about ten feet deep. The miners and I went down to the bottom. There was a little lead matter, but we didn't think there was a wall. At my suggestion, the miners dug about the wall, which proved to be nothing but a single boulder about three feet in diameter. After some digging, the boulder rolled into the bottom of the shaft. That exploded the wall theory in the Cumberland No. 2 shaft.

After much sparring to the Court, the evidence was closed and the arguments began. McConnell's argument was really masterful, but the closing argument by Will Wallace overmatched it. Judge Henry charged the jury, which found for the plaintiff, Riggs.

The defendant moved for a new trial on several grounds, among them an alleged irregularity in the jury. One of the jurors was Charles Ladd, a very good man, who lived at Neihart. I was sent to Neihart to obtain his affidavit. This was in early December, 1891.

I rode the stage to Woolsey's, half way, then changed to a sled. The road went over King's Hill, the highest point over which a mail route then ran in the United States. The mountain is high, the road being cut through the pines for a long distance. Seeing what I thought were blaze marks on the trees, I asked the stage driver why it was that the blazes were so high above ground. "Them ain't blazes," he replied, "them's singletree marks."

The trees were seventeen feet above the ground and that winter they went to twenty-one feet. As the snow fell in the road and was beaten down, it gradually raised the road above the ground. This indicated the deep snowfall on that mountain. If a horse slipped off the road, he was likely to be lost for months. On a road near Woolsey's during that winter, a horse had slipped off the road and fell down the hillside to the little valley, about thirty-five or forty feet, and there he stayed until spring. There was no way to get him out. The stage company fed him hay and he ate snow for water. Probably the horse was grateful when a chinook came.

Neihart was a large mining camp in a deep canyon. The sun was not visible more than three or four hours a day in December. The principal hotel, the Frisco, was like the one in Castle; its front door opened on the sidewalk, and the rear of the second story abutted on the mountain. It was a mountain in Neihart, a high hill in Castle.

I soon found out that Mr. Ladd had gone to Great Falls, so I followed him. There was a railroad, or a kind of one, running from Great Falls to Neihart. For a distance it ran through a box canyon.

This was my first visit to Great Falls, but I had passed through on the Montana Central going to Michigan. I suppose it was a city of 3,000 at that time, but it had some imposing buildings, one of which was the Park Hotel, at which I stopped. Mr. Ladd was there and I got his affidavit. Then I went back to Neihart, where I spent the night.

A NEAR MISS WITH FROZEN FEET

The next morning I took the sled. It was the usual sled with high box sides. The inside, which we would call the tonneau now, presumably was for mail, bottled beer in cases, beer kegs, groceries, packages and what have you. The seats were high—too high for one's feet unless there was baggage of some kind. On this cold morning, there was nothing in the "tonneau" and my legs were without support; they hung from the knees down. This stopped the circulation to some extent, enough so that my feet were soon cold. I knocked them together, but that didn't help much. After a while, they ceased to hurt. The sled reached Woolsey's. I got out stiffly and walked to the house.

Mrs. Smith, a comely young woman, asked me if I was cold. I said no, but my feet had been cold and weren't anymore. She said, "Sit down in that chair!" As I did so, she took off my left overshoe and then my shoe. Rolling down my sock disclosed a frozen foot as white as marble. The right foot was much the same. She called to her husband and gave him a large dish pan, which she told him to bring her at once full of snow. She explained to me that we had to work fast, as they could not keep me overnight. I just had to go with the stage.

She seated me at the table with both feet in the snow, and I ate my dinner with her, her husband, and the driver. After the meal, Mrs. Smith examined my feet again, but there was no change. She said she would keep the driver as long as she could. Before long, she pinched my feet and a faint sign of blood under the skin appeared. Putting my feet back into the snow, she went into her bedroom, returning with a pair of red wool socks she had knit. Turning them inside out, she sprinkled plenty of red pepper in them. Wiping my feet dry, she pulled on the wool socks, the red pepper next to the skin. Then she put on my overshoes, giving my regular shoes to the driver, who had hitched the horses to the stagecoach.

"Now," said my benefactor, "you've got to walk ahead of that stage to the top of the ridge, and that's four miles. Then you can get on the stage. When you get to town, go to Billy McGinness's and get some witch hazel, none of this Pond's Extract. Get some cloth that will hold the witch hazel and wrap your feet in it. Sleep with your feet bound that way for three nights, and I don't think you will ever have any chilblains."

It was pretty hard walking to the top of the ridge ahead of the stage, and my feet, as far as feeling, might as well have been in a fire. But coming into White Sulphur, they began feeling pretty comfortable. I did as I was told, and in three days, my feet were entirely normal. I have never had the dreaded chilblains.

GIVEN UP FOR DEAD

I had another even more harrowing experience in the out of doors while I lived in White Sulphur Springs, and it just happens that it occurred in October. My friend Austin Gormley and I went hunting together. He and I, Byron Whitney and George E. Anderson drove a team high up on the North Fork of the Smith River. After making camp and spending the night, Austin and I started out together and became separated in an unfamiliar country. Used to mountains, I went further than he did and, familiarity breeding contempt, foolishly failed to observe the landmarks carefully. I might as well have been a tenderfoot. It was a country in which old residents frequently lost their bearings.

Going over a ridge, I found deer signs and came upon a deer. I shot at and missed him, or suppose I did. Rushing after him, I failed to find him and could not get back to my trail. It began to snow and my glasses became clouded. I sought landmarks, went to hilltops, climbed trees. I went up an old road that led long ago to a sawmill. Then I found a trail going up a hill. I passed some cattle and they took after me, a big black steer with long sharp horns in the lead. I ran up the trail until out of breath, the cattle after me, then sat down and made up my mind if they came much closer I would kill the black steer and while the herd was bawling about him I would escape. But fortunately they stopped. The truth was they belonged to a famed outdoorsman named Jake Hoover who had befriended artist Charlie Russell when he was newly arrived in Montana. Jake's cattle were gentle; to them a man meant salt and friendship. Deer visited the salt licks and Hoover always had plenty of deer meat. If I had had sense enough to keep on that trail, I would have come out at Hoover's cabin by nightfall.

As it was, I realized "our camp was lost." So I took the old timer's way and started down a stream. It was the north fork of the Judith; fortunately it was not the Lost Fork. Soon I got into deep tangled timber that was some four or five feet deep. Realization soon came to me: if you fall and break a leg, you will die. So carefully I went to the stream and followed that a long way, until dark. When darkness came on, I walked ashore and, luckily, landed in a little flat where there were some dead willows, but they were wet and it was turning cold. The night passed. I had shot the head from a grouse and the grouse toasted over the fire was my supper, not a very good one. I had my watch and wound that. A good part of the night I put in watching the dipper, the sky having cleared. If one knows how, one can tell the time by the dipper as well as he can by the sun.

In a little while there was a terrible screaming in the canyon, like a woman's frightened shriek. This, I suppose, was a mountain lion. About the break of day a bear came near me; I pointed my Sharps at him but the bear had no hostile intentions. He was hungry and wanted some ants for breakfast. He turned over an ant hill and ants swarmed on his paws. He licked them off, and by and by went into the timber.

As soon as it got light enough to travel, I got into the creek and followed it. After a time I noted the canyon narrowing and came to a waterfall, maybe ten feet high. The walls of the canyon were so precipitous I could not climb them, so I jumped over the waterfall, getting as wet as McGinty who "went to the bottom of the sea." My gun was dripping, but from then on I had good walking on the left side of the creek. That was welcome because with so much walking in the water I had blistered the tops of my toes, and were they sore! My trouser legs were worn from my calves to the bottom. It was a fine sunny morning but I was tired and very hungry.

I walked and walked and finally saw three log cabins in a group. Now, I wondered, what would I do if they were deserted? But going further I saw one of the most pleasant sights of my life—smoke coming from a chimney. It was the home of Jake Hoover in Pig Eye Basin. Below the basin, canyon walls reddish in appearance lowered on either side. If I had not found someone at Hoover's I would have had a tough time indeed. As I approached the house from which the smoke was coming some dogs came around the corner barking and then Hoover showed up with a frying pan in his hand. As soon as I came within speaking distance he said, "Young feller, who are you?" I tried to say good morning but I croaked. My voice was gone from exhaustion or drinking too much water. Hoover wanted to know from whence I came, and, as soon as I could get my voice, I said, "Down in that canyon," and he said, "You look it." But then he said, "That cannot be so because the canyon is impassable. There's a waterfall there." I told him I knew that because my clothes were hardly dry yet.

He asked if I were hungry, and I said, "You bet." He yelled into the house to put on a "frying pan of meat." He had three women there, but I never knew the relation. I ate all the deer meat they served to me and it was a frying pan full. I drank two or three cups of coffee and felt good. Hoover wanted to know how far I had come. I traced my steps as well as I could from our camp to Pig Eye Basin, and he said in astonishment, "Why that's about sixty miles!" which was perhaps an exaggeration. But it was far enough. I told him I must go back at once as the boys would get to worrying. He gave me a saddle horse and told me the way, warning me to be careful when I reached the top of the divide. I started out on an easy trail which led to the hillside where I had seen the cattle. It was a short cut.

When I reached the divide upon which was a growth of timber, pine and quaking aspen, a terrific storm was raging, lightning striking all around, and close by, thunder roaring. I carried my gun on the saddle, across my legs. One might have feared to do that, as lightning was striking so close, fifty feet at one time, but I had no fear. My trouble was sight. Snow obscured my glasses and my lone handkerchief was sopping wet, not much better when I wrung it out.

The first I knew we were going downhill, shortly into a canyon along a stream. We went through timber, some of it down, but nothing like the down timber of the day before. About nightfall I came to a wood chopper's cabin and told him my story. He said I was on the north fork of the Musselshell and could not go on until daylight. He said he was sorry he had a narrow bed but he guessed we could manage to sleep together. Supper was about ready. It consisted chiefly of some sort of a split pea mulligan, but you may be sure I ate a hearty meal. Why he didn't have meat I couldn't figure out; he lived with it all about. I had come through it all afternoon, but since I had no way to save the meat, I didn't shoot. We went to bed. It was narrow but I had a sound sleep. The wood chopper said he slept as well as usual.

After some kind of porridge for breakfast the wood chopper gave me directions to the Nagues ranch. Hoover had told me to leave the horse with someone on the north fork of the Smith River, but leaving it with Nagues was just as good, so that's what I did. I walked to our camp, arriving a little before noon. No one was there. I wrote on the lid of a cartridge box that I had arrived at 11:00 A.M. and had gone hunting. I went up the little creek Austin and I had followed when starting to hunt. The ascent was heavy and I was approaching the head of the creek where the willows were small, not over four or five feet high, on the right bank going up, when I looked across and saw Austin. He was standing still, leaning on his gun. I said "hello" but he did not move, so I helloed again. Then he came slowly toward me looking at me steadily. When within four feet he held out his right hand and as I took it, he said solemnly, "I never expected to see you alive again."

We returned to camp. My absence the first night did not alarm my partners particularly but when I had not returned by 11 o'clock the second night, "By" Whitney got on a work horse and rode him bareback to White Sulphur Springs. His arrival caused considerable excitement. Dr. Kumpe, the coroner, and a dozen men left for the north fork of the Smith River at once. They arrived at our camp about an hour after I arrived. Dr. Parberry was arranging for a party of forty or fifty to leave soon if I was not found. It was thought I might have perished in the heavy and unusual electric storm which was visible from White Sulphur. Of course there were numerous conjectures about me. I was lost, that was certain. Perhaps I had been in a bar fight, maybe I had broken a leg. Prayers were offered in the churches for my safety. I related the incidents of my adventure to my hunting mates and the coroner's party, perhaps with too much levity, for "By" Whitney felt that I did not appreciate his strenuous efforts in my behalf. That was not true; I was grateful to the bottom of my heart for the solicitude of my friends, including Jake Hoover and the woodsman who shared his food and his narrow bed with me.

MY FRIEND AUSTIN GORMLEY

Now is a good time to tell more about my special friend, Austin Gormley. When I first came to White Sulphur Springs, Napoleon P. Smith had as a law partner a young man who was not doing as well as Mr. Smith expected, and he dispensed with him. Smith then sought me out and said, "I would like you to come in with me, but I would not ask you to leave Mr. Waterman, but don't you have someone in mind you can recommend? Maybe you have in mind some classmate." I then showed him the photographs of three of my classmates at Ann Arbor, among them Austin C. Gormley. Mr. Smith seemed inclined toward Austin, and I told him he would make no mistake in choosing him. He asked me to write to my friend, which I did.

Austin came in good time and the firm of Smith & Gormley resulted. It was opposed to Waterman & Callaway in many cases. I had become a member of the latter firm in November, 1891. The two firms were together sometimes. As I remember now, their joint efforts were almost invariably successful.

Austin and I went to parties together, took out the girls together, and, as we have seen, went hunting together. As we shall see later in this narrative, he was my best man when I got married. While a Montana born boy and reared chiefly in this Territory and state, Austin knew little of the outdoors. He was born into a family which was overtaken by poverty, although his father was a man of many excellent parts. Austin as a boy, youth and young man had worked at the printing trade; he did so in Ann Arbor. Nevertheless he kept up his studies well and took lessons in elocution. He had native oratorical ability, and won for Michigan first place in the Interstate Collegiate contest in 1891 with his oration "quo warranto."

Austin was popular with both men and women. He was twice elected County Attorney of Meagher County, moved to Great Falls and was elected Cascade County Attorney. Before he was elected to the latter post, an incident occurred that eventually brought him into state prominence. William Gay and George Gross, brothers-in-law, were suspected by the people of Castle of thieving and other felonies. We had a suit for slander in our office in which Gay was the plaintiff against a number of Castle citizens.

Someone in Castle swore out a warrant for Gay and Gross for grand larceny. It was placed in the hands of Bill Rader, a deputy sheriff, for service. I knew Bill well. As Gay and Gross had fled into the hills, Rader and two or three others went to arrest them. Gross shot Rader from behind, killing him instantly. When Rader's body was brought to town I was standing on the sidewalk in front of Boungard's undertaking shop. As the wagon backed violently against the walk, Rader's body shot out into my arms.

The death of Rader caused great excitement. A large party gathered to capture Gay and Gross. I wanted to go but Mr. Waterman talked me out of it. Finding I was not going, a young man borrowed my chaps and joined the party. I never saw him or the chaps again. The party followed Gay and Gross down the Musselshell. The fugitives were hiding in some timber as the party filed past. James Mackey, a member of the posse, unfortunately spied Gay as he lay in the timber, watching, and Gay shot him through the middle, fatally.

Afterwards Gay was captured at Needles, California, and brought to Montana for trial. Gross was never captured. It fell to Austin Gormley to prosecute Gay, who was defended by Colonel W. F. Sanders. A change of venue was granted from Meagher to Lewis and Clark, and the trial took place in Helena, attracting statewide interest. The prosecution by Gormley, and especially his closing argument to the jury, was masterful. Gay was convicted and hanged.

Austin continued to rise in public favor and if he had lived he would have been elected U.S. Senator in a few years, without doubt. One summer, he went to White Sulphur Springs to visit his wife, who had been Irene Spencer, and while there was stricken with appendicitis. Dr. Brooke was summoned from Helena but a hard storm made the roads nearly impassable. While waiting for Brooke, the White Sulphur physicians did nothing except to alleviate the pain, and Austin died.

I could not write my memoirs without telling of Austin Gormley, my dear friend, or omitting to narrate the odd occurrence that follows: On the day Austin died I was mowing the grass in my yard at Virginia City with a scythe, gathering it with a rake and pitchfork. The scythe was lying on the ground. I was leaning on the pitchfork thinking. Before my eyes swam the picture of the scene on the north fork of Smith River. It was as clear as when it happened. I saw Austin coming to me and heard him say, in memory, "I never expected to see you alive again." Just then my wife stepped out on the front porch and said, "Lew, you are wanted on the telephone, long distance." I thought nothing of that; being District Judge I was often getting long distance calls. As I took the call, someone, I think Sid Spencer, Austin's brother-in-law, said from White Sulphur Springs, "Austin Gormley has just died." I felt faint. I had arranged to go to the Madison the next day fishing with my wife and Tommy Monaghan, my stenographer, and his wife. We went, I thinking it would mollify my feelings. On the way back, while the team was tugging up the ridge, I told Tommy this singular occurrence and of the peeve "By" Whitney seemed to entertain after my hunting adventure. The next morning in the Anaconda paper I read that Byron Whitney had been electrocuted in his bath tub in Butte at just about, if not exactly, the time I was telling the story to Tommy Monaghan.

I thought to, intended to, go to Great Falls to Austin's funeral, but regret to say that I had not the courage to do it. I was sure I would make a disgraceful spectacle of myself, which would make the situation dreadful at the best, worse for Irene and Austin's mother. I knew my feelings would not be understood by anybody. So I remained at home and mourned my friend.

CORRECTING A MISCARRIAGE OF JUSTICE

I had two more White Sulphur Springs cases I want to relate something about. Max Waterman defended a man of Finnish descent whom the people of Barker (or maybe it was the people of Neihart), were determined to hang. Mr. Waterman was convinced the man was telling the truth, and that manslaughter was the most the man was guilty of. By skill in trial work and oratory, Waterman saved the man from a verdict of murder in the first degree. Instead the jury found him guilty of murder in the second degree. Some years later, one of the eyewitnesses who testified at the trial, being on his deathbed and stricken with the pangs of conscience, signed a sworn statement which showed the slayer's story was true, and the man was pardoned from serving further. I helped Waterman in my feeble way.

The next year, Mr. Waterman was retained to defend one Peter McDermott. Will Wallace was to assist him, and I sat in the trial with them. McDermott, a miner with powder marks showing on his pale face, had been confined in jail for some months. He looked like a criminal. McDermott's sad story was that while he was working in the mines, one Bill Murain had seduced his wife. This coming to the ears of McDermott, a decent man, he talked it over with his wife. She confessed. With her consent, Murain was sent for. He came and McDermott said to him, "Mary has told me what has happened between you, and I want to arrange this peaceably," or words to that effect. Murain, a large man, jumped to his feet, towering above McDermott, and snarled, "Mary is a G— D— liar." McDermott drew a revolver and killed Murain where he stood. Then McDermott made a great mistake: he fled the state. Years later, he was captured and thrown in jail.

Despite the efforts of Wallace and Waterman, the jury found McDermott guilty of manslaughter, and Judge Frank Henry sentenced him to ten years in the penitentiary. All of us who were involved in his defense, including Will Wallace, were always certain that Judge Henry had made a mistake in dealing with this basically honorable man who had suffered so much from his own foolish mistakes. We gave notice of intention to move for a new trial and applied for bail. Judge Henry placed it at $10,000.00. P. H. Maloney

(Jack), a leading saloon keeper, cursed the Judge, but set to work to raise bail and after great efforts succeeded.

During the trial I had taken copious notes, having learned how to do it in college. Getting a true transcript from the official stenographer in good time we thought impossible. So Mr. Wallace and I set to work to get up a motion for a new trial based on my notes. We worked all of two nights and all the third until 3 o'clock in the morning; then we went to bed, for we needed some rest.

We served the motion and the prosecution did not propose any amendments. The motion was submitted to the Judge, who took it under advisement. When court convened the next term he granted it; he said the court had given an erroneous instruction. The case was set for a new trial immediately. McDermott appeared, and he was a different looking man, brown and healthy in appearance. We went to trial, and the jury acquitted McDermott in six minutes. It was a triumphant moment for us.

6

PERSONAL HAPPINESS IN WHITE SULPHUR SPRINGS

A Cold Winter

Coping With Financial Panic

Woodson Badger and I Go to the World's Fair

Back to Work and a Girl Named Nell

Notable Hunting Adventure in 1893

In February of my second winter in White Sulphur Springs came the coldest weather I ever saw. On February 5, 1893, I wrote my mother a letter in which I said, "Monday the thermometer went down to 52 degrees below here in town, and at Fort Logan, twenty miles below here, the government thermometer froze up at 60. It warmed up Tuesday to 24 degrees below, and that evening went down to 52 certainly, some say 54, and two self registers showed 60 below Tuesday night. Wednesday night it was 49 below. Thursday was cold. Friday it warmed up and we thought a chinook was coming. Thermometer reached 50 degrees above! Last night it began to fall again and at 9:30 this morning it stood at 24 degrees below. Altogether it beats anything I ever saw. I milked Mrs. Waterman's cow and by judicious use of mittens did not get my hands cold. Mr. Waterman frosted his nose, and Miss W. while sleighing with one of her fellows frosted her nose and left cheek. As it is her left cheek I have a joke on her."

During the cold spell I made a fire in the little "box" stove in my room, putting in red fir because that lasted. One night I put in a round red fir stick. The next morning frost was all about and my breath congealed as I exhaled. A pail of water on the stove had frozen, bulging up in the center. It took nerve to get out of bed to fix the fire. Finally I did so, and there was fire on the bottom of the round stick. Fire in the stove and water frozen in a bucket on the stove! Telling that story, the truth, when I went uptown earned me the reputation of being an accomplished liar.

A man came over from Neihart and was taking a drink in Jack Maloney's saloon. He said, "I hear you been having some weather over here." "Yes," was the reply, whereupon the man said,"We had it 79 below in

Neihart." "79 below!" a bar patron roared, "how do you know that? No thermometer in this state registers that low." "Well," said the man, "a mule freezes at 79, and one froze to death in Neihart."

COPING WITH FINANCIAL PANIC

In 1893 the national financial panic came on with all its startling developments. It was customary for people in White Sulphur to deposit every cent they had in the bank at night and draw it out in the morning. The bank received deposits up to 5:00 P.M. One morning the bank didn't open. I had a silver dollar in my pocket and that day was one of the richest men in town in actual cash. The only time I ever was rich.

Creditors made a rush to collect their accounts. The poor debtors were in worse trouble. For me it was a satisfactory period. I didn't pay my room rent, didn't pay for my board, didn't pay for anything, hung onto my silver dollar. Mrs. Hartfield, who kept the boarding house, the best I ever saw, didn't pay the grocer who didn't pay the wholesaler; she didn't pay the butcher who didn't pay the cattleman; and everyone locally was happy. It was a big joke.

Some wholesale concern back East became panicky about an account owed by Thomas Noble at Big Elk, sixty miles from the Springs, sending the account to our law firm with directions to attach at once. I made inquiries of the bank, whose officers spoke well of Noble and his fine stock. I talked the matter over with Mr. Waterman, and with his approval I hired a team and drove to Big Elk. It was a hot day, and dusty, the horses soon tired, and when I whipped them into a trot, every revolution of the wheel spilled clouds of dust in the buggy. Finally we made it.

Noble kept a stopping place in connection with his business. I told him the situation, and we agreed to go over the books in the morning. I was tired and went to bed immediately. The place was new and had clean beds. I wasted no time in going to sleep, and did not wake until a man shook me violently at 4:00 the next morning. It was a Mr. Neihart, one of the discoverers of that camp. When he saw me open my eyes and heard me speak, he said, "Excuse me, I thought you must be dead; how anybody can sleep with these bed bugs is beyond me. I been fighting them all night and you haven't moved. Look at my sheets!" His sheets were a shambles. I had moved because I had killed bed bugs in wriggling around. But I went to sleep again and didn't get up until around 6:00. Bed bugs don't bite me, but I don't like to feel them crawling.

Noble had a fine, clean stock, owed little, had a good business. He made a small payment and promised more. I got in the buggy and drove to White Sulphur Springs. I wrote to the company, sent them the collection less fee, and told them Noble would pay if let alone. Otherwise they might lose. They cooled down and we got them their money.

Some time later a hoodlum called Australian Bill got drunk and took a shot at Noble. Powell Black was the County Attorney. He filed an information charging Bill with assault and the information was good. Noble wanted the Australian prosecuted, and he employed me to help the County Attorney, stipulating my fee. My services being acceptable to Black, with whom I was on good terms, we prosecuted Australian Bill together and convicted him. Noble gave me my fee and wrote out an additional check for $25.00, saying, "This is for you. I know you have got to divide the other with Waterman. This is for that speech ye made."

WOODSON BADGER AND I GO TO THE WORLD'S FAIR

Woodson Badger and I became firm friends, and during the summer of 1893, we played tennis together a good deal. He told me that his uncle, John A. Woodson, then the largest sheep grower in Meagher County, was going to ship a train load of sheep to

Chicago and maybe we could go along and thus see the World's Fair, the Columbian Exposition. The more we thought about it the more eager we were to go. The papers were full of the wonders of the Fair and occasionally someone who had been there would attempt to describe its marvels.

I had $60.00 and could get $25.00 more. Woodson, by discounting his next warrant for his monthly salary, could raise some money. So we "struck" Uncle John for a job. He said we could go, and on October 9 we left White Sulphur Springs for Livingston, where the sheep were to be loaded, I driving two horses hitched to a spring wagon. We reached a ranch not far from Livingston, where we spent the night, driving to the town in the morning.

Then we had to load the sheep. The cars were double-deckers and the train consisted of twenty-three cars. Tommy Hampton, the young man with us, and Woodson had had some experience with sheep but this was my first. Of all the stupid animals in the world I think they equal, or surpass, them all. But finally they were loaded. Mr. Woodson bought a rake handle for each of us; with this implement we were to poke the fool things if they got down to where their fellows could smother them. Every time the train stopped we would get out of the caboose and run along the train to see if any sheep were down.

The train men paid little attention to us. At one place sheep were down and we couldn't get them up, so Tommy got inside. Just then the train started and we had to lock the door on him, and he rode with the sheep until the train stopped again. The train men didn't wait for us and started up, so we had to climb up the car sides and run along the tops of the cars, jumping from one to another, in order to reach the caboose. On one occasion I was almost at the front of the train when it started. Climbing up the first car available, I ran along the tops toward the caboose but the train got up so much speed I found it dangerous to jump from one car to another. So I sat down on the end of a car and hung onto a brake wheel until the train stopped. The wind was blowing and it was cold. I was pretty miserable when the train stopped.

We unloaded at Sunnyside, three miles this side of Mandan, North Dakota, to give the sheep time to feed and water. Then we had to load the pesky things again. We ran to St. Paul, and then to Trevor, sixty miles this side of Chicago, where the sheep were to be fattened for market. And after all this, Mr. Woodson got about fifty cents a head for his fine wethers.

Woodson and I, being told what to do, had taken along a complete change of clothes in a steamer trunk which we carried from one train to another. We had been sleeping as best we could in the caboose, eating at the stations where the train men did. At Trevor we changed to a passenger train used for the purpose of taking sheepherders and the like to the Union Stockyards in Chicago. We got into a Pullman car so called; it was said to have been one of the first Pullman cars built and I believe it was. It had little resemblance to the Pullmans of today. Arriving at the stockyards, we were told to carry our steamer trunk to the hotel at the stockyards, to take a hot bath, throw everything away, including the shoes we had worn on our trip, put on fresh clothes and shoes, get a haircut and shampoo. We also got a shave, but even after all that, I smelled those sheep for a week.

Leaving the stockyards, we went into Chicago, looking for a place to stay. We wanted something cheap and got it, fifty cents a night. It was in a building that had once been a store, a stairway leading from one floor to another. The rooms were divided by thin partitions less than the height of the room. The ceiling over the partitions was of "chicken wire." The acoustics in the room were startling; if a man sneezed anywhere in the room, every lodger heard it.

The Fair was uppermost in our minds. Someone told me in going to the Fair to go by boat on Lake

Michigan. This, he said, would permit us to land at the Lake end of the Court of Honor, which was the most spectacular view to be had. We would go out by rail, he said, the straightest way, after taking our first trip by water.

The Court of Honor from our landing was the most beautiful spectacle, created by human hands, that it has ever been my good fortune to see. I stood thrilled to the core, as did Woodson. We did not speak for a while. Eventually we walked toward the other end of the lagoon, where John Philip Sousa's band was playing. After listening to the music we went into the various buildings in which the multitudinous exhibits were shown, finally ending with the Midway Plaisance.

I have been to other Fairs, notably the one at St. Louis ten years later, and the Century of Progress forty years later at Chicago, but neither equalled the Columbian Exposition in beauty or interest. There was so much to it: a magnificent midway with carnival shows like Buffalo Bill's Wild West, exhibits of the very newest in Pullman cars, new industrial inventions, electric light bulbs, and replicas of Christopher Columbus' three ships. All of this was housed in the "White City," built on the swampland of Chicago's East Side, which, according to its builder, Daniel H. Burnham, was the "miniature of an ideal city built as a unit on a single architectural plan . . . a symbol of regeneration."

We felt regenerated all right, but also tired, after spending every night at the Fair and in Chicago until we were well-nigh exhausted. In about a week, I persuaded Woodson to go with me to Tuscola, Illinois, for a visit with my relatives, who must have thought we were two pretty stupid boys. We could not get enough sleep. Even I, who to this day can't sleep in the daytime, did so then. The visit concluded, we went back to Chicago for more Fair.

We ran out of money, and had visions of being in a

great city broke. While in this impoverished condition, I was walking along the sidewalk in front of the Marshall Field store early one morning when who should I see but Alex Wetzel from the Ruby Valley! I remember the incident that bright morning very well. Mr. Wetzel was as surprised as I was. He had a cigar stuck between his teeth which, upon seeing me, he threw into the gutter, exclaiming "By Jacks!" and holding out his right hand. After a little talk he asked if he could do anything for me. I said yes, I was broke, could he lend me $25.00? He said, "Yes, come down to the bank with me." Woodson found some friend from Meagher County and got a small loan. So now we were in funds, not enough for more fun at the Fair, but enough to see us home.

We bought a berth on the Pullman and rode back to Townsend in style. At that point, we found as a passenger a Miss Black, a dressmaker of White Sulphur Springs, and we there hired a "rig" to go home, stopping at the Half Way House for a late supper. Woodson and I had a few cents left so we went to the saloon and bought something the bartender called a cocktail. There was nothing like it in Chicago! We were pretty tipsy, but Miss Black said she would not tell our girls in White Sulphur Springs about it. We didn't tell her we had no girls, but in fact we didn't. We reached White Sulphur late at night, in good health and spirits, having enjoyed the greatest experience of our lives up to that time.

BACK TO WORK AND A GIRL NAMED NELL

The next day, Woodson and I went back to work, he in his father's Clerk of the Court office, and me in the law office of Max Waterman. Things went on pretty much as before. Shortly after that I began to take Woodson's sister, Nellie, to parties. I had seen her occasionally before that. When I arrived in White Sulphur in 1891, she was about fifteen years old. Of course I knew her father and her brother even better by then. I had also met her mother, who had been Miss Frances Lathrop Woodson as a girl. Her husband called her Fannie, or Fan.

The Woodsons, from whom Nell was descended, were a prominent family in Missouri, and were well known in Kentucky as well. Their family traces to Virginia, as my own family does. I learned that Nell's mother was a direct descendant of Dr. John Woodson and his wife, Sarah. Dr. Woodson was a surgeon in a British regiment sent to guard the colonists. He and his wife had landed at Jamestown in April, 1619, on the ship *George*.

Nell's maternal grandmother, Amanda Dick Woodson, also lived in White Sulphur Springs when I first met her, and she was a most remarkable woman. At that time she was living with her daughter, Mrs. W. R. Baker (Aunt Emma). Later she lived in California with the Badgers after they moved there in later years. In 1910, Amanda Woodson was past 99 years old, still retaining all her natural faculties except her sight. She had been blind for 50 years, the result of the experimentation of a blundering doctor.

Amanda was a girl in the days of Daniel Webster and Henry Clay, and she used to read their speeches to her father. Having a prodigious memory, she not only could remember the substance of the speeches of these great men but, at the age of 99 years, could recite cantos of Milton and had a brain filled with quotations from other poets whose works she had read as a young woman. Mrs. Woodson died at Riverside, California, at the age of 100 years, five months and sixteen days.

Living with the Badgers in White Sulphur at the time I first got to know Nell and her family well was Judge Badger's mother, whose name was Buell. She also was a fine woman. She was "quality," and I remember my father always referred to her as "an elegant lady."

It was evident, early on, that Nell came from a remarkable family, and, as the reader will perceive along the way, Nell was remarkable herself. She was going to school when I began going with her. I used to help her in translations of Caesar, but I think she didn't remember much of the Caesar I helped with. The courtship progressed so satisfactorily that we became engaged on December 27, 1893. From that time on, our romance took up much of my thoughts and doubtless interfered with my work. Winning over Nell's parents to her marriage at such a young age was another matter.

NOTABLE HUNTING ADVENTURE IN 1893

Before I got engaged to Nell, I went on a memorable hunting trip in the Fall of 1893 which I would like to relate. The party consisted of Austin Gormley, Lee Southmayd, Woodson Badger and I, and our hunting grounds were in the Lake Creek country. It was an interesting region. We wandered over the extinct volcano, examined the lava flow, and walked over the solidified glassy flow, which reminded me of the material in the obsidian cliff in Yellowstone Park. It was a well watered country with grouse all along the streams. We pitched camp along a fine little stream and caught some fish. Austin was willing but he didn't know how. "How do you clean these fish?" he asked. When we killed grouse I saw him sitting on the bank of the stream picking the feathers from a grouse. I laughed and said, "What are you doing that for? You don't pick a grouse, you skin him." He shot back, "My mother picks chickens." "Yes," I said, "and she singes them too." The next day we all went hunting. On the top of a mountain, Dr. Southmayd became separated from the party. As the rest of us got to the bottom we began to yell "Lee!" but got no response. After a little we fired our guns, which brought an answering gun shot. Then we heard, "Where are you?" "Down here," we replied. After a while we hollered, "Where are you?" He shouted, "Right down here at the bottom of the hill." He couldn't have been far away, for we heard him yell, "Right down here is a hell of a big country!"

Shortly he showed up, and in going near a quaking aspen grove we found grouse, which caused the party to separate, some going on one side and some on the other. As we were coming close together, I saw Lee jumping in the air shouting, "Don't shoot!" Austin was shooting at grouse directly between himself and Lee, and he did the same thing when I was in line, the shot falling all about me. He seemed to think the shot would stop with the grouse.

That night a man whom I had known in Madison County, Elmer Burger, came to camp with us; so now we had a party of five. The next day Woodson and I went deer hunting. I took my Sharps and he carried a Winchester. We hunted hard all day. Just as we had left a trail through the timber and stepped into a park, a small deer trotted out of the trail and stopped. I was so startled that I fired over the deer, which jumped down the hillside and escaped. About sundown we saw four or five deer playing in an open place. They were running around like calves but were too far away to hit, unless by a rare accident, and we didn't shoot at them.

We realized we were high on the mountain but we didn't know how many miles from camp. The lovely mountain twilight was upon us, but we didn't have time to sit down and enjoy it. We knew darkness would shortly be upon us, so we began our descent and soon it was dark. Coming to a rocky hill, we groped our way down, holding onto the rocks until we came into a little narrow valley. It was pitch dark now and we stepped with caution. That is a steep country. All of a sudden, it seemed something big and black moved into the trail ahead of us. Bear, we thought. We saw it move; now what to do? The hillsides were steep and climbing them might lead us into danger. I cocked my Sharps and I suppose Woodson did the same with his gun, and we courageously moved right into that bear, which was a bush. Our imagination made it move.

We kept going down the valley, then to our relief we saw a big red moon. It was a full moon, and the smoke of a heavy forest fire made it red. The smoke from that fire overspread the country for many miles. The moon to our left gave us our bearings, and by keeping it to the left and rapid walking, we saw our campfire pretty late that night. Austin, Lee, and Elmer were sitting around the fire, worrying about us. After narrating our adventures, it was time for all to go to bed.

Mary Elizabeth Link Callaway, c. 1872

James E. Callaway, Montana Territorial Secretary, 1871–1877

Montana Historical Society Photograph Archives

Llewellyn Link Callaway as a young boy, Virginia City

The James E. Callaway home in Virginia City, built in 1875

Montana Historical Society Photograph Archives

Virginia City, Montana Territory, 1877

Montana Historical Society Photograph Archives

Wallace Street, Virginia City, 1877

Lew Callaway as a recent graduate in law

Montana Historical Society Photograph Archives

MONTANA GRADUATES, UNIVERSITY OF MICHIGAN, 1891

Lew Callaway and Dr. LeRoy Southmayd and Austin Gormley, two of his closest friends, are seen in this picture of 1891 Montana graduates from the University of Michigan at Ann Arbor. In the back row, left to right: Austin Gormley, lawyer; Dr. Noyes of Butte; H. S. Hepner, lawyer, Helena; Geoerge Denton, dentist, Red Lodge. Seated in the front row, left to right: Julian A. Knight, lawyer, Twin Bridges; A. A. Zimmerman, graduate in literature, later superintendent of the Asarco Refinery in East Helena and the donor of this picture to the Montana Historical Society; Ernest Cullen, graduate in literature, formerly of Helena, later of Spokane, Wash.; Dr. LeRoy Southmayd, formerly of White Sulphur Springs and Virginia City and later of Great Falls; Lew Callaway of Virginia City, graduate in law.

Montana Historical Society Photograph Archives

White Sulphur Springs, Montana, c. 1892

Ellen (Nell) Badger Callaway, 1913

Lew Callaway, the busy new Madison County Attorney, was photographed at his desk in about 1895.

Montana Historical Society Photograph Archives

Madison County Courthouse in Virginia City

Nell and Lew Callaway, seated left and right, with their two oldest children, Miriam and Jim. In the background are an unknown young lady and Grandmother Mary Elizabeth Callaway.

Nell Callaway holding infant son, L. L. Callaway, Jr., as sister Frances stands by in Virginia City, winter of 1907.

Nell Callaway, left, joined two of her close friends in Virginia City in 1910 for an afternoon of diversion. In the center is Mrs. Julian Knight, whose husband was a University of Michigan classmate of Callaway, and at right is Mrs. Sam V. Stewart, whose husband was a fellow lawyer in Virginia City.

Nell Callaway seated on the front steps of her home in Virginia City in about 1912 with daughter Miriam beside her and daughter Frances in the background.

Jim Callaway sits with his young brother, L. L. Callaway, Jr., in Virginia City, 1910

The Callaway children photographed in Berkeley, California, in 1910. Left to right: Miriam, Jim, Frances, and L. L. Callaway, Jr.

7

BACK HOME TO VIRGINIA CITY— WITH A POLITICAL FUTURE

A Fourth of July Oration and a Hiatus at Home

A Tantalizing Offer

White Sulphur Springs Friendships Remembered

Successful Campaigns For Office and For Marriage

The Wedding

Dr. Lee Southmayd, who had been in partnership with a Dr. Craig in White Sulphur, moved to Virginia City in January or February of 1894. He and I had continued our close friendship. He did not sit around and waste his time as young doctors frequently do in a small town. He studied, took excellent care of his patients, and experimented. For instance, he wanted to know more about how to treat a patient with a perforated bowel. He acquired an "ornery" dog, and with my help, cut the dog open and perforated a bowel. This he did after administering ether to the dog. I was the anesthetist. It seemed to me it took quarts of ether during the perforation and subsequent treatment. He sewed up the incision and the dog licked it out. The funny thing about it was that the dog loved us to distraction. Maybe he liked the ether. He got well anyhow, perhaps from the licking.

After Dr. Southmayd had been in Virginia City for some weeks, he wrote me that the committee in charge of the Fourth of July celebration wanted me to come and be the orator of the day. I accepted, wrote and learned my speech.

When the time came, I went to Townsend by stage and found the American Railway Union had closed down the Northern Pacific Railroad, as it had most of the railroads in the United States. It had been my intention to go from Townsend to Norris by train, but that was not to be.

I hired a team and driver to take me to Sappington, which was then a busy stock shipping place in Gallatin County on the spur line of the Northern Pacific that ran from there to Norris, which was the end of track. We drove all night from Townsend to Three Forks, a dark night in the rain. It was so dark that we could not see the road except for the rain standing in it. Shortly after daybreak, we came to the Jefferson River, which was running high. The descent from the hills to the bridge in that damp early morning with the odors of the roses and other wild flowers, the trees and willows, was lovely.

This road led to the old town of Three Forks. There was a large hotel in the place, and we were growing sleepy. Some rooms were locked and some with beds in them were unlocked. Being unable to arouse anyone, I took a bed in one of the unlocked rooms, as did my driver. We got up about 7:00 in the morning and still there was no one about. So we went down the street to get something to eat. There was no restaurant, as an early-rising storekeeper told us, and there was no eating place at the hotel. He said we might not be able to find any proprietor at the hotel before 9:00 or 10:00. So we bought some crackers, cheese and sardines for breakfast and went on to Sappington. I have always wondered to whom we were indebted for our rooms at the hotel.

I said goodbye to my driver at Sappington. Somehow I got to Norris, but the stage had gone. I hired a saddle horse which I rode to Virginia City, practicing my speech along the way. I sent the horse back to Norris by stage the next day—he was tied behind.

My folks were glad to see me. After a good night's sleep, I went over to "Injun Rock" and in solitude said my speech once more. This was on the morning of the Fourth of July. At the appointed time I delivered it to the "assembled throng" at the Courthouse in Virginia City. People seemed to like it. The speech over, I enjoyed the festivities of the Fourth and went to the ball that night.

My father, who was nearing 60 years of age, was not in robust health in 1894, and was doing little work at his law office. As a result, I knew the family was hard up, for my mother had told me so, once saying it would help if I could only send her $5.00, which I "wangled" one way or another.

There were some things in the office I could help with, and I went there every day, doing some little work. My brothers were growing up—Edmund was fourteen and George eleven—but they weren't much help. I did what I could around the house, too, as I found little things to do. My father's health gradually improved and he lived another decade, but these were hard times.

A TANTALIZING OFFER

After having been in Virginia City about a month, I received a letter from Mr. Waterman asking me to come back to White Sulphur because he had to go to Iowa on business. In the meantime, friends had been talking to me about running for County Attorney of Madison County. I refused, pointing out that I was a resident of Meagher County. They said that legally that didn't make any difference, and as William Alexander (Will) Clark had held the office for three terms and was generally disliked, even hated, I would win in a walk. I should add that this W. A. Clark was not the famed Copper King, but rather a man who, like me, was a graduate of the University of Michigan Law School, and eventually served as a State Senator from Madison County. He was my continual irritant through many years.

But back to the matter of running against him in 1894: Considering the condition of the family and the state of business at White Sulphur Springs, I told my friends before leaving Virginia City that if the convention nominated me I would make the race. We had John, a horse broken to buggy, and my friend John Conway loaned me another, so I took the buggy which had been purchased in the early 1870s and the buggy harness, hitched up the two horses, and drove to White Sulphur Springs.

I knew the road, for I had ridden my horse Firefly

from Virginia City to White Sulphur in 1893. Incidentally, I rode Firefly about White Sulphur a great deal, keeping him in Waterman's barn. But the expense becoming too great, I put him out to pasture. After I went to Virginia City to live, Ed Hall, long of the law firm of Gunn, Rasch, Hall & Gunn, asked if he might ride Firefly to Lewistown, where he thought he would practice law. I gave him permission. Someone stole the horse from Ed, and I never again saw the best horse I ever owned.

Getting back to White Sulphur Springs: I went into the office and worked diligently until Mr. Waterman returned. The greatest pleasure in returning was that it gave me opportunities to see my girl, Nell. My absence had been irksome to both of us because the railway strike left us without mail communication for weeks at a time.

In September I received a telegram saying the Madison County Republican Convention had nominated me for County Attorney. After a conference with Nell, we agreed to be married if I were elected. This was not taken kindly by Judge and Mrs. Badger, who thought Nell was too young. She was eighteen years old in August. We thought she was not too young, and we said while we wanted her parents' consent, if I were elected we would be married, consent or no consent.

I had a piece of business on Reese Creek in the Gallatin Valley to attend to for my friend, John Reed, of Virginia City. John was an old-time placer miner and capitalist by now. I drove the buggy from White Sulphur Springs through the Flathead Pass to take care of this matter. It proved to be an adventure.

The buggy didn't have any brakes, and the hames wouldn't stay on the horses' collars on a downgrade. The result was that the buggy would run into the horses, which would try to hold it back. The hames would shift onto the horses' necks, and then the harness would slip under their tails! All I could think of to do was cramp the buggy wheels, something of a feat on the mountain grade, put the hames back, straighten the harness, and try it again. All things come to an end, and finally we got down to the floor of Gallatin Valley.

After attending to the business, I drove to Bozeman, where I stopped for a few hours. While hitching up in the afternoon, William L. Holloway, a young lawyer, came to see me. He said he had been nominated for County Attorney of Gallatin County, and since I had received a like nomination in Madison County, he would send me the returns from his race as soon as he got them if I would do the same with my returns. Of course I said I would do that, and we shook hands, wishing each other good luck. I was to see much of that young man in after years when we both served on the Montana Supreme Court.

WHITE SULPHUR SPRINGS FRIENDSHIPS REMEMBERED

While I lived at White Sulphur Springs, I came to know well everybody worth knowing and some not worth knowing. But most of them were. For instance, in town there lived David E. Folsom, and, ten miles out, Charles W. Cook. These men were both early Montana miners and stockmen who in 1869 mounted an expedition to explore the wonders of Yellowstone. They were accompanied by a third man, William Peterson, a ranch hand employed by Folsom.

Folsom was a native of New Hampshire and studied civil engineering in college. Before finishing his course he was compelled to leave school because of poor health. He went west, joining the James L. Fisk train of 1862 headed for the Salmon River gold mines. He became the hunter for the party. He spent the winter of 1862–63 in Bannack, then went to Virginia City and eventually to Diamond City and White Sulphur Springs.

After his trip to the Yellowstone, Folsom wrote a

faithful narrative, but publishers would not accept it, one writing him that his publication no longer accepted western fiction. Finally the *Western Monthly Magazine* of Chicago published the article. Men who knew Folsom believed the truth of what he said and set up such an agitation that the Federal Government was persuaded to send out an official expedition under Montana Territorial Surveyor General Henry D. Washburn.

Members of the party included Lt. Gustavus C. Doane from Fort Ellis commanding a military detachment. Civilians included Nathaniel P. Langford, former U.S. Collector of Revenue for Montana and later the first Superintendent of Yellowstone Park; Cornelius Hedges, Helena lawyer and first territorial Superintendent of Schools, and Samuel T. Hauser, president of Helena's First National Bank and later Territorial Governor.

This historic expedition became known as the Washburn-Doane Expedition, and it resulted in Yellowstone becoming the nation's first National Park in 1872. Probably the impetus of the idea came from Hedges. At the party's camp near the junction of the Firehole and Gibbon Rivers, there was a debate around the campfire. One of the party talked of homesteading some land to embrace the geysers. Hedges rose and declared that the whole region should be proscribed from settlement; that it should be set aside for the benefit and enjoyment of the people. Those words are engraved in the arch at Gardiner.

Langford seconded Hedges' idea vigorously. The result was that Territorial Delegate William H. Clagett in Congress introduced the bill which, upon adoption, established Yellowstone National Park. Mr. Folsom became a wealthy sheep owner, was Senator from Meagher County, and the Republican candidate for Governor in 1900. He was in our office frequently and I got to know him well.

I also came to know very well William Parberry, a

client of the office, a man I have already mentioned as the one who laid out the town of White Sulphur Springs. He was a very forceful man, a doctor by profession, by now retired. Probably he was the richest man in the county. He was the first State Senator from Meagher County.

Dr. Thomas M. Hampton had dental offices adjoining Mr. Waterman's law office. A door entered from Waterman's to mine, and this proximity led me and Dr. Hampton into frequent contact. When he was about to administer laughing gas to a patient, he called upon me to assist him. He did not consider it safe to administer the gas without assistance, a witness at least. After some experience, the wisdom of the course was plain; I saw some funny demonstrations. Occasionally a patient would dream, do and say some outrageous things. Tom Hampton and I became good friends, and as of this writing are still friends in Helena, where he practices dentistry.

Before I take the reader to Virginia City and the beginnings of my life there, I would like to mention some other men I came to know well in White Sulphur Springs, most of them favorably. Mr. Waterman was on friendly terms with Spencer, Mayn & Heitman, and I got to know the members of this law firm well, too, especially Louie Heitman. They had a clerk, Richard Manger, whom we all called Dick. We became very good friends. Dick was a poor boy, but diligent and faithful in his service. Eventually he became a considerable figure in the industrial life of the county.

Other young men of White Sulphur Springs who were active in business and social life during my time there were James T. Wood, Cashier of the First National Bank and later State Senator; Charley Wight, my helpful friend in the County Clerk's office; Harry Giltiman, afterwards a member of the Legislature, as was Charley Sherman, also a friend in White Sulphur. Others I would mention include David Penwell, Dan MacKintosh, George Wiltse, Dick Collins, Ned

Peckham, and of course, Dr. Lee Southmayd and my future best man, Austin Gormley.

I also counted as friends William T. Ford, father of Willie, a boy destined to be District Judge and a good one; George Wallworth, Sheriff Charley Rader, Alfred Bumgard, and William H. and Bob Sutherlin, editors of the *Rocky Mountain Husbandman.* And as related earlier, there were B. W. Badger and John A. Woodson, whose families I would join by marriage.

SUCCESSFUL CAMPAIGNS FOR OFFICE AND FOR MARRIAGE

I started campaigning as soon as I entered Madison County. My father had written advising me to do this, at the same time giving me the names of some of his friends. Cherry Creek running into the Madison River in the canyon was about the line between the two counties. In those days it was the custom to stop your team and talk unless you could see the other person was in a hurry. It was different from these days when you go whizzing past your best friends, who do the same.

I talked with several whom I met in the canyon, stopping overnight in Red Bluff, then still a pretty active mining camp, although nothing like it was in earlier days. Now it is a ghost town, apparently uninhabited. Except for the Tanner Hotel building, now vacant, a newcomer would not know it had been the site of a booming gold mining town and the strategic midway stop for stages traveling between Virginia City and the Bozeman area. I attempted to "make some medicine" with the dwindling numbers of Red Bluff inhabitants, and the returns showed that I did.

When I got to Virginia City, I agreed to campaign the county with Jake Albright, who had been nominated for County Treasurer. I was to furnish the team and buggy, and we were to "go halves" on the expenses.

Jake had been a clerk for R. C. Hickman, famous early day merchant of Virginia City, and Montana's first State Treasurer.

Jake Albright had an unusual faculty for remembering names and faces, and he had an attractive personality. His company was fortunate for me. We agreed that we would campaign without whiskey. Others had tried it and failed, and some of our friends doubted the wisdom of such a course. We made, or tried to make, a house-to-house campaign of the county. My father said that if I went to a man's house and did not see him to write him a note at the next post office telling him I had called to see him. This was good policy, and I followed it.

There was one thing we had to be careful about, and that was the fight for the State Capital. Everyone was talking about it and the feeling was intense. A man would ask, "How are you on the Capital?" If you answered Helena, or Anaconda, you might lose a vote. Jake and I agreed we wouldn't tell, and we didn't. Neither of us knew how the other intended to vote to the very end of the campaign, although I think we might have guessed. Once in a while a voter would say, "If you don't tell me how you are going to vote on the Capital, I don't see how I can vote for you." I would answer, "I'm not campaigning on the Capital issue. If you don't think I have sense enough to vote right, I guess you'll have to vote against me." That usually fixed him. I never directly asked anyone to vote for me. I should add that I wrote some editorials in favor of Helena which were published in the *Madisonian*.

It seemed that every miner we encountered had been in Virginia City and had met Jake and Jake knew him. I first saw this in the town of Pony. We passed over the site of Sterling, once an important town, but now practically gone. Only a few old-timers can point out where it was. At Pony I noticed that the people were very friendly and that my opponent, Will Clark, was very unpopular. Jake seemed to know everybody and of course introduced me. We went on to Sand Creek, a small camp, which was reputed to be strongly Democratic. But even here, Jake found friends, most of them miners. I met them all. Then we went through Summer Valley, Democratic, and South Boulder, Republican. I met people in South Boulder, farmers and ranchers, who became my friends for all time.

I shall not take the time to tell about all our stopping places, but there was an incident about a mile north of Twin Bridges that was unusual. We saw a man chinking a cabin inside a field perhaps a hundred feet from the road. I drove close to the fence and stopped the team. We yelled "hello," but the man disregarded it and we helloed again. Finally he came to the fence and said, "What are you fellows grinnin' about? You must be runnin' for office. Throw your jug in sight." We said yes, we were running for office and introduced ourselves, but we didn't have a jug. "No foolin'. Now I want to see your bottle," was his retort. We said we didn't have any. He said, "How in hell do you expect to be elected in Madison County without packin' whiskey?" We said we had resolved that we wouldn't carry any whiskey, and we hadn't, and offered him a cigar. He said no, he didn't smoke. "I reckon you are Republicans," he said, to which we said yes. Then, surprisingly, he said: "I'm a Democrat and I never voted for anybody but a Democrat, but if you fellers are makin' a campaign and ain't packin' whiskey, I'm going to vote for you. I went to a dance up at Rochester in 1868, got drunk and made a fool of myself. I ain't drunk any whiskey since, and I ain't got any use for a man that does." We thanked him and drove on. When we got to the towns, of course we had to treat in the saloons, a custom that I always hated. I hate the saloon business, and as a rule have no use for saloon keepers and bartenders, but there have been a few exceptions.

We of course campaigned Twin Bridges, Leiterville, a mining camp, and Sheridan thoroughly. I was nominated under the name Llewellyn L. Callaway. I protested to my father that the name Llewellyn would lose me votes. He said nonsense, that every Welshman and Cornishman would be for me because of that name. This I found to be true at Leiterville, a large camp named for the mine owners, L. Z. and T. Benton Leiter. Right away the first Welshman I met said something to me in Welsh, which I couldn't understand, and pronounced my name Welsh fashion. And so it went. Every Welshman was for me enthusiastically, and every Cornishman was friendly.

When it came time to go upon the Upper Ruby, I told Jake I would have to break our rule and take a jug because it would be threshing time. He said all right. This was political wisdom. Before we reached the Valley, some campaigner was being denounced because he hadn't carried a jug, and some friend of mine said, "Wait until Lew Callaway comes along; he'll have a jug." I carried the Valley 4 to 1, and there were a good many votes.

Election day was exciting. Clark had been spreading lies of many kinds about me. A damaging one was that in Adobetown and Laurin I was an A.P.A., short for American Protective Association, a radical anti-Catholic secret organization then growing in strength nationwide. In Pony, on the other hand, I was a Catholic. Some boy I went to school with rode up from Adobetown saying they were accusing me of being an A.P.A. and that it would lose me votes. I got on my horse, Jailbird, and sailed down to Adobetown. I said the report was a lie. I was a Mason and didn't deny it, but I was not and never had been an A.P.A., nor was I. I carried Adobetown 2 to 1. But I could not reach Laurin and I didn't get many votes there.

At Pony they had investigated, and when Clark's helpers began to spread the report that I was a Catholic, the A.P.A.'s there set to work. I carried Pony by a 97 majority out of 160 votes, Virginia City 2 to 1. The returns were slow in coming in. The night we got the last one, from Lyon, which went 7 to 1 for me, I received a postal card from Will Holloway saying, "Dear Callaway, I am elected by 415 majority. Yours, Holloway." I bought a postal card and wrote him, "Dear Holloway, I am elected by 415 majority. Yours, Callaway." Correction made my majority 412.

THE WEDDING

As a result of this campaign, during which I had won the office of Madison County Attorney at the munificent salary of $100.00 a month, Nell and I agreed to be married on December 12, 1894. There was no further objection from her parents. My mother said we could have the two upstairs rooms in her house in Virginia City.

The house looked shabby, so I determined to paint it before the wedding. I bought some white lead and some vegetable coloring matter, making the paint cream colored, with maroon trimming. I was astonished to see how thirsty the boards were. They took up the paint as if they were sponges, it seemed to me. I did all the painting myself except for the very highest part in front. It was too high for me. When the house was finished, it was handsome.

In due time, I went back to White Sulphur Springs for the wedding. When a girl is making preparation for a wedding, with the help of her mother and girl friends, there is no room for a man. He is a nuisance, and actually, in general estimation, he seems to rate lower than the best man. As related earlier, my friend Austin Gormley was my best man. I think neither of us understood the mysteries of the goings on.

Eventually the great day arrived. The bride was to be married in a going-away dress. She was pretty in it. In fact, she was pretty: five feet five inches tall, brown eyes that sparkled, dark brown hair, and red cheeks. We got up at four o'clock in the morning to the tune of Judge Badger hammering beaten biscuits. I dressed with care, putting on my Prince Albert suit.

The wedding was at 6:00 A.M., the Rev. J. A. Hedges, a young Presbyterian minister, officiating. Then followed a wedding breakfast at the long table at which the entire family was seated: Judge and Mrs. Badger, Woodson, Dick, Emma, a girl of nine years, and little Jack, with the best man and Ella MacKintosh, the bridesmaid. It was plenty sentimental.

It was a cold morning, zero, and we had made preparations for the stage journey to Townsend. Each of us had a fur coat—the bride wore a man's coat, borrowed from Harry Giltiman—overshoes, and something about our ears. At the Halfway House we had lunch. The only thing about it that I remember is cornstarch pudding in blackberry juice. We expected to take the train for Helena at Townsend, but it was late. It didn't reach Townsend until 8:00 the next morning, so we had to put up with the "bridal suite" at the Townsend Hotel. And that, no surprise to me, was roughing it.

The next morning we took the train with avidity and ate breakfast in the dining car. Reaching Helena, we registered at the Helena, the best hotel in town at the time. Our Helena friends were kind to us. The first night we were there, Chad Spaulding, a young stenographer-lawyer with H. D. McIntire, and his new bride took us to dinner at a restaurant. Mrs. Samuel Word took us young folks from the country to their grand mansion for lunch, and for a drive in her carriage, the coachman presiding, to the Broadwater Hotel, then in its pristine glory. When we came back and the carriage stopped at the *porte cochere* at the Word mansion, we thought we were tasting of high life for sure. Coming back down to earth, we realized we had little money and had to be going, so we took the train to Butte, where we had shopping to do without any money.

I had bought a carpet, in the Fall after my election, for the double room in my parents' house in Virginia

City. It was a Wilton velvet, which cost over $100.00, on credit. It was a kind of golden brown. That carpet at this writing is where it was first put down, and it doesn't show much evidence of wear.

So far the wedding trip was pleasant. We stayed overnight at Butte, but the train to Whitehall was late, so we missed the stage. I employed Ed Wolverton to take us at least to Twin Bridges. We started out in a spring wagon, which broke down ten miles out, at Fish Creek. We sat there for an hour or two, and it wasn't warm, while Wolverton went across the Jefferson River by the Parsons Bridge and borrowed a lumber wagon. We reached Twin Bridges about dark, having decided to stay overnight.

As Ed was unhitching, one of the horses kicked him and broke his leg. There was no doctor in Twin Bridges, but some men set the bone and put on some home-made splints. Someone made a wooden support for the leg, which looked like part of a sluice box. This they rested on the wagon seat and dashboard and put a pillow on it. The next morning, I lifted Ed into the seat with his leg on the pillow, and he drove from Twin Bridges, to Whitehall, thirty miles. We found a young lady in Twin Bridges who lived in Virginia City. With her as a passenger, we hired a spring wagon and drove to Virginia City, arriving shortly after noon on December 18. My mother was not expecting us until evening and was cleaning the house. When she saw me, she in her work clothes, she said, "Don't bring that girl in here," but made a rush for Nell.

Thus I arrived in Virginia City with my bride ten years to the day from the time I started for Philadelphia as a 16-year-old to go to prep school. We lived in my mother's house for seven or eight years. Miriam and Jimmy were born there. My mother and my wife were two unusual women. They lived together in harmony, despite the saying that no house is big enough for two families. To the end of her days, while my mother had three daughters-in-law and liked them all, Nell was her favorite.

8

BEGINNING LIFE IN VIRGINIA CITY

Social Times and Recreation

A Gratifying Mining Experience

We Start Our Family

Great Hunting and Fishing

Houses and Buildings of Virginia City

After the Christmas and New Year's festivities, I went to work practicing law. Besides the $100.00 a month I received as County Attorney, I also picked up some income through some civil business. Life in Virginia City was pleasant, despite some drawbacks. My wife and I were happy as young lovers should be. My mother gave a reception to the young people of the town, who thronged the house.

Nell and I had a room on the second floor of my parents' house, and were happy even in our restricted quarters. I took her with me to the Upper Ruby and the Madison River fishing, and to Butte. We went to parties, to the balls and ordinary dances. Nell would dance until the last number was called, but having to work the next day, I frequently wanted to go home early.

The young people organized a dancing club which met in "Armory Hall," one of the large business places of Virginia City's early days. It had been a store, first occupied, I believe, by C. E. French, a grocer. The upstairs had been occupied by the Masonic Lodges years before, and the Grand Lodge of Montana had been formed there in 1866. The spot is now marked by the Masonic Monument.

This dancing club was what it was designed to be: a place where young married people and the young unmarried people of the business type could enjoy themselves in a wholesome atmosphere. The club was sociable, friendly, fun-loving, and generous. There was nothing "snooty" or "exclusive" about it. The members were good dancers, some of them excellent. As suggested earlier, my wife was among the latter, and she loved to dance. It was a pleasure to watch her. Some of the older people came occasionally, mostly to sit by and look on.

In June, 1895, Benton Leiter, who was managing his uncle's mine at Leiterville, invited the young people of Virginia City to celebrate the evening of July 3 at the mine, he to bring his men to Virginia City the next day for a drilling contest and a tug of war on the Fourth.

My wife and I went to Leiterville in an open one-seated buggy, one horse, via Sheridan. From that town to Leiterville it was eight miles up Wisconsin Creek and the mountain. The funsters said it was eleven miles up and eight miles down. About fifteen couples finally arrived, the ladies sleeping in the manager's house and cabins and the men wherever they could; mine houses, stables—anywhere. It was a tough night on the boys after the dance was over.

The dance was held at the dining hall near the mine, a mile up the steep mountain from Wisconsin Creek. Preliminary to the dance there was an elaborate and extensive display of fireworks, which could be seen for many miles. Something set fire to the powder house where the dynamite was stored, and as it turned out, there was enough dynamite to blow away the entire mountain side. Incredibly, Leiter's miners went into the powder house and carried out the boxes of powder, one by one, some blazing, until the fire was out! It was an heroic exploit, indeed, and despite the danger, contributed even more excitement to an already exciting night.

As I recall, there was a tramway running from the mine to the mill, about 3,500 feet below. Some miners rode down in the tramway car, but we from Virginia City preferred to go down on the road on foot even if it was a mile. Breakfast in the morning was late, and new to the visitors: smothered spicy chicken and champagne. No one present ever forgot that breakfast.

As agreed, the Leiter crowd showed up in Virginia City for the Fourth, and there was a classic old time celebration in the mining camp. The ringing bells, roaring cannon, and the staccato explosion of firecrackers ushered in the day. Foot and horse races, drilling matches, the struggling giants in the tug of war (won by Virginia City), all made the day lively. The Grand Ball in the evening finished the festivities.

As winter came, we coasted down the snowy streets, and took part in social activities. In those days the Masonic fraternity was still holding its St. John's Day banquet and dance and children's party.

Later on, the Virginia City Dramatic Company was organized, trained by two former actors who evidently had enjoyed considerable activity in that profession. We played *Our Boys*, *Rosedale*, and other high class plays, and some not so high class. The troupe did so well with *Our Boys* that it was taken to Sheridan where it played with acclaim from the citizens. Later David E. Bandmann, world famous actor, and his wife, a former actress, played what Bandmann called a Shakespearian "Olio" with the aid of our club, and also a play, *David Garrick*, which was popular in its day.

Bandmann chose me to play Mr. Jackson, the second character, he taking the role of David Garrick. It was during this play that I received a lesson from him that repaid all my efforts on the mimic stage. I did not speak properly and did not know why. I told Bandmann there was something wrong, and I wanted to improve my delivery. We were rehearsing *David Garrick* at the time. Bandmann said, "Read your lines and I will observe you." Going to the exit used by the public, he gave me a signal and I commenced reciting my part. Walking slowly to the stage, he raised his finger, saying, "Open your teeth." I was having trouble with enunciation. After that the trouble disappeared. From then on, I spoke clearly and distinctly, filling large halls without difficulty.

A GRATIFYING MINING EXPERIENCE

Among the people I came to know in Virginia City, Nathan D. Johnson will always be fresh in my memory. His nickname was "Chunky." I have a snapshot of him taken when he was a Justice of the Peace in Virginia City. He was 6 feet 4 inches tall and weighed some 256 pounds. He had been a member of the Legislature in 1871, and possessed one of the finest legal minds I ever encountered. While he was not an educated man, still he had gone to school and was by no means ignorant. But he had been in the Wild West since boyhood, had been a hunter and guide. Of keen mind and retentive memory, he was one of the best story tellers I ever knew. And here I kick myself. If I had not been so busy with trifling things, like drawing deeds, chattel mortgages, contracts, and the like, but had stopped to take notes of Chunky's stories of the old West on various topics, I could now be drawing a good income from some of our leading magazines relating stories as Chunky told them to me.

I tried many cases before Chunky in the Justice Court. He understood the necessity for the "cold neutrality of an impartial judge." Many of his rulings would have done credit to a District Judge.

Physically, Chunky was lazy; indeed, his great frame carried so much weight that this was to be expected. He had done much prospecting in his time, and much representing, so he said. His representing work consisted mainly of a fine outing in the mountains on a lovely Montana autumn day.

Out of this prospecting had come the May mine, "the best damn mine in the mountains," according to Chunky. Fall after Fall, he was gone representing the May. But one season he was laid up with the gout and could not get out in the high country in which the mine was located.

Along in December, Chunky came into my office saying he feared that, after all his hard work, he was going to lose the May. Some of those "loafers," he said, had been watching him for years, getting ready to jump his claim. A day or two later he came into my office, lamenting his hard luck. He was laid up with this gout, had no money. The thought of those men jumping the May was just more than he could bear. Would I consent to locate it? He would rather have a friend get it if he had to lose it.

The next day he enlarged on his idea of my relocating the May. He said he knew a good man, Joe Deraet by name, who would do the development work in the tunnel where the discovery ore was sticking out of the walls, and put up the corners. I wouldn't have to wallow around in the snow, and it wouldn't cost me but $65.00 or $75.00. Thinking I would be throwing that much away, I told him, all right, I would do it. We chose the name High-Up for "the best damn mine in the mountains."

Chunky had married a widow with three daughters, the youngest of whom married a man named E. W. Merritt, a "mining man." Some time after the High-Up was a valid claim, Chunky came in the office saying Merritt, his son-in-law, would run the tunnel on the High-Up a number of feet further into the mountain for one-third interest in the claim, and that work should develop the ore body. I told him all right, let Merritt go to work, but the work must be first class and the tunnel well timbered. When the work was done, and well done, Merritt might have his deed.

As I was making out a mining deed conveying a one-third interest to E. W. Merritt, it struck me that it would make Chunky happy if I gave him a like interest, and I made out a like deed to him, chuckling as I did so. Seeing County Clerk Henry Steffens going by at about noon, I asked him to take the acknowledgments of my wife and myself to the deeds, which he did. When Chunky came in to get the Merritt deed and I gave it to him and also the one made to him, he was overcome. He sat down and remained silent for a while and then said in a choked voice, "Lew, I never expected this," to which I replied that if the mine was as good as he had said, there was plenty in it for all of us.

Some weeks later Chunky drifted into the office, saying that his son-in-law had a man from Duluth interested and he wanted a lease and bond on our interests in the High-Up. "Well," I said, "let's give it to him. What price shall we put on it?" Chunky suggested $5,000.00, at which I hooted. I said, "You used to say that the May was the best damn mine in the mountains, and now you are willing to lease and bond a two-thirds interest in it for $5,000.00. Go jump in Alder Gulch!"

"Well, $10,000.00 then," Chunky said, and I agreed. I would draw up the papers, and I did this: I made the $10,000 payable in installments, payable at different dates, with six percent interest on all sums not paid when due. I was pretty certain the payments would not be paid on time, and they weren't. I recall getting a check for $250.00 for deferred interest. When I gave Chunky a check for $125.00, he inquired what is this? And when I told him he said he had been paying interest all his life, and this was the first ever paid to him. He was going right down to the Pony saloon and buy a bottle of champagne.

We kept extending the time for payments. The upshot was that we received $10,500.00 for our two-thirds interest in the High-Up. Chunky's half kept him in comfort for his remaining years, not very many, and there was enough left to bury him decently. This High-Up incident has given me great satisfaction; it is a pleasant recollection.

WE START OUR FAMILY

About January, 1896, probably before that, my wife and I were made aware that a great event was coming in due course, and on July 6, 1896, our first child was born. We named her Miriam, and she was a little beauty. As she learned to talk, it was seen that she had a high order of intelligence. During the Spanish-American War, when she was two years old, I would take her downtown, and she would astonish the grown-ups with conversation about the war. Her grandparents were inordinately proud of her, but her parents, foolish young people, were too strict with her; they wanted her to be perfect.

GREAT HUNTING AND FISHING

And so life in Virginia City ran along happily for the most part. Superb entertainment for me, which I often shared with my family, was the hunting and fishing which in this vicinity was unbelievably good as we look at conditions today. The Madison River was the greatest grayling stream in the world and it was inhabited also with trout and white fish, so called. The trout were mostly native, but Rainbow and Loch-Levin or German Brown, began to propagate. Some of the younger men, like Lewis Kiser, Lee Southmayd, Jim Powell, Henry Steffens, Zack Clem and I would leave Virginia at 4:30 or 5:00 in the morning, drive over the mountain to the Madison, begin fishing at about 9:00, and have something like sixty fish apiece by 1:00 P.M.

Before the power plant was built on Blaine Spring Creek, two men could catch forty or fifty trout there in a morning, early in the season. Another favorite stream was O'Dell Creek, then full of Eastern Brook trout. It was good the year round. Perhaps the "sweet-est" stream of all was the "right hand fork" of the Ruby River early in the season. The camp was between the "right hand" and middle forks, and the fish were nearly all native trout with a few adventurous white fish. I would catch fifty or sixty fish between 9:00 in the morning and 1:00 in the afternoon. The fish were small, say from seven to ten inches. We would cook twenty or more of the small ones in a frying pan and eat them, bones and all. They were delicious.

Fishing was good in the middle fork and in the "left hand" fork, but the latter was difficult because of brush conditions, including scrubby pine trees. It was fine fishing in the river formed by the union of the three streams down as far as the canyon. There were some holes that were close to an angler's dream. The scene was picturesque, made so by the mountains covered with trees, the clear stream, flanked with willows, rushing from one bank to the other into the deep holes. The fish were plentiful and hungry.

On one trip to Three Forks, the party being made up of Jim Powell, Johnny Rodgers, Billy Hustead, Rodney Herndon, and myself, we caught many fish and had an unusually good time. Rodgers grew angry whenever he caught a white fish, and autocratically made a rule that no one must bring a white fish into camp. Wild game was close about, including bear. Rodgers had a fine outfit, an expensive rod with all the fixin's. He and Rodney went up the right hand fork ahead of me; I was perhaps 200 yards behind them. As I was catching fish steadily and was absorbed in the fun, I did not pay any attention to Rodgers and Rodney. Suddenly I heard an uproar which at first seemed to be a combat, and I wondered if they had run into a bear. But out of it came loud swearing of intensity, punctuated by Rodney's high tenor laugh. Rodgers had hooked a double, but they were both good-sized white fish, and had broken his fine pole. Back at camp, Rodgers was still mad, and Rodney said he had never seen such a demonstration in his life.

Some years I took my wife and children to Three Forks and we all caught fish and enjoyed a lovely outing. It was pleasant to camp out with good tents, plenty of grass, wood and cold water. Our beds were on the ground, sometimes softened with pine boughs and willows. If we caught too many fish, there were friends in town who were glad to have them.

One day late in August, however, we met an unusual condition. When we arose, the clouds were down upon the Snow Crest Peaks, a north wind was blowing, and snow flakes were in the air. We had agreed to have flapjacks for breakfast and carried out the plan. The snow flakes sizzled as they hit the hot griddle. Generally conditions were uncomfortable. We got breakfast as fast as we could, "rustled" the horses, and went down the river. I remember that on this trip, besides Jimmy, we were accompanied by Neil Brantly, son of my close friend, Theodore Brantly, perhaps the greatest Chief Justice that Montana's Supreme Court ever had. But back to our trip that cold day in August: the north wind continued to blow, and we were thankful when we reached the Brook Nook for a belated lunch.

The upper Ruby was still a fair location for hunting, but the elk were gone. The mountains east of the Madison, though, furnished fine hunting. The country was extensive, extending to the Gallatin River. Indian Creek, Taylor's Fork, Lightning, Cache, and other streams were wild in their upper reaches. Mountain sheep were in the Taylor peaks, which are over 11,000 feet high. Anywhere around the Sphinx, called by some Mount Washington, or Red Mountain to the north, east or south was fine hunting country, especially Shedhorn Mountain.

A trail from Bear Creek, a tributary (sometimes) of the Madison, led over the mountain to Indian Creek, and thence to Cache Creek, a tributary of Taylor's Fork. Famous elk, called "Old Yellow Horn" and "Clubfoot," were constant lures. These bulls ranged close to the Sphinx.

HOUSES AND BUILDINGS OF VIRGINIA CITY

Nearly all the houses in Virginia City were frame, some log, and a little later, some brick residences were built. The Madison County Courthouse, built in 1873–74, was brick. The city hall, built in the 1890s, was also brick. On Wallace, the principal street of the town, some of the business places were of stone, quarried near the city. Elling's, Ward's, Gilbert's, Gohn's, Thaxton's, a later creation, were all built of stone.

Practically all the houses had no inside "toilet" conveniences of any kind. All householders burned wood, which cost $8.00 a cord. The stoves accordingly were wood burners, the old fashioned kitchen stove, box-burners, and the more elaborate wood stoves for the living room. After coal was available, because of the closer advent of the railroad, the Cole's Hot Blast heater was popular. But nearly everyone had cold water in the house; the water came from mountain springs, and it was good. After coal came into use, pipes were run from the kitchen stove to a tank and we had hot water. This was a luxury to anyone who had never had it except as it was heated in a "reservoir" in the stove or in tea kettles.

We were troubled in winter with the freezing of the water pipes, which sometimes burst. We were short of water for our lawns in summer. Our markets were none too good, but the merchants did the best they could.

The automobile has changed the hunting and fishing conditions in Montana. Fishing is not what it once was; gone are the big catches I once knew. But the automobile with its comforts, and the good roads it has brought into being, have greatly alleviated the asperities which beset the pioneers.

9

ADVENTURES OF A NEW COUNTY ATTORNEY

Struggles to Set Up an Office of Law

A Maniac and a Murder

A Rich Man and Tainted Beef

Vindication of a Fledgling County Attorney

In 1895, the Madison County Commissioners bought me a Smith Premier typewriter, and I learned to use it. But they would not buy any books, and I had only those which the State furnished—the Statutes of 1887 and some earlier, and the laws of 1889, 1891 and 1893. My predecessor, Clark, the man I had defeated for the office, had a good library. But in his meanness he had printed some signs which he posted all over his office: "No person is permitted to examine or take any books from this office under any circumstances." I knew this meant me; it couldn't mean anyone else.

I just had to have some books, and so I purchased sixty-three volumes of the California Reports on the installment plan. With the Montana Reports, furnished by the State, and the Californias, I got along until I could buy more. On July 1, 1895, the Montana Codes came into effect, but we had nothing except the paper Codes which were recommended to the Legislature by the Code Commission and we did not know whether the Legislature had adopted them *in toto* or not. We knew they had adopted them with amendments but where were the amendments? It was sometime in the Fall before the Codes with the amendments came out in their sheep-bound covers.

A MANIAC AND A MURDER

The absence of these laws put me on the spot about July 1, the day they were to go into effect. George F. Parker, the local giant, with whom I had gone to school, came running down the gulch, his long legs flying, in early July—I think before the Fourth—early in the morning. Rushing into a saloon as the swamper was in the midst of his work, George, who never drank, burst out: "Terrible thing happened up the gulch this morning, father killed mother; give me some whiskey!"

The swamper placed a bottle on the bar with a large whiskey glass. George filled the glass full and drank its contents, and went raving crazy. He had been crazy before, had been sent to the Asylum at Warm Springs, and had returned, apparently cured. The swamper told the first man he saw what he had heard and seen, and soon the report was all over town. The sheriff and I and some other men went to the Parker place. George's father, Nahum Parker, was there but wouldn't talk. Mrs. Parker lay on her bed, shot in the temple. It was a ghastly sight.

George, a maniac, was put in jail raving, and he continued to rave. Dr. McNulty, the coroner, puffed up with his authority, held an inquest. Nahum Parker swore he knew nothing of the facts except that he heard a shot, and found his wife dead.

In a calm interim, George was brought from jail. He was cunning and parried the coroner's questions. The coroner could not get him to commit himself on anything. He (the coroner) resented any assistance from me; but when an *impasse* was reached, I said, "Doctor, let me ask him a question or two." Since he gave no sign that he had heard me, I turned to George and said: "George, do you know who shot your mother?" "I didn't say that anybody shot her." "I know; I didn't ask you who shot her; I asked you if you know who shot her." "Yes, I know who shot her; I shot her myself," and with that, George went into a maniacal demonstration and was taken back to his cell.

The coroner's jury found that George Parker killed his mother. I did not believe it then and never have believed it, but I did not know who the murderer was. George continued to grow worse if that were possible. At my suggestion, fortified by the opinion of Doctor Hagan, we finally devised a way to restrain him. Joe Haines, the sheriff, ordered Fred Kraemer, the saddler, to make a harness by means of which five or six of us, using our utmost strength, fastened George's hands to the outside of his legs, and thus kept him from injuring himself or anyone else. While we were doing this, he was trying to bite us. To keep his mouth busy, someone put the bone handle of a case knife between his teeth, and he bit on it savagely.

Dr. Hagan said we must commit poor George to the Insane Asylum as soon as possible. I examined the paper-covered Codes and found that the commitment must be made by the District Judge, who was at his home in Boulder. I wired Henry J. Haskell, the Attorney General, asking him if the paper Codes contained the law on the subject, or had it ever changed? He answered that the Legislature had adopted the proposed law without change.

In the meantime, I had wired District Judge Montgomery H. Parker to come at once, which he did. The method of committing an insane person was new; perhaps this was the first commitment under it. Under the terms of the law, the authorities had to follow a prescribed course: a complaint had to be filed, a warrant issued, witnesses subpoenaed, two physicians summoned who were required to make certificates to the District Judge who was required to make an order of commitment reciting certain facts. It was as new to the Judge as it was to me, but by following the Statute, the law was not difficult of administration. I drew up all the papers and George was committed to the Asylum at Warm Springs. His name was George Farnsworth Parker.

Imagine my surprise when I received a letter from the Attorney General, saying that he had been advised that one George F. Parker had been committed to the Asylum, and that if this hadn't been done or that hadn't been done, reciting the jurisdictional requirements of the Statute *seriatim*, the sheriff of Madison County would be required to forthwith present himself to the Asylum and take the said George F. Parker therefrom and convey him to the county jail of Madison County, and so forth.

I was mad. I sat down at my Smith Premier and wrote the Attorney General a letter in which I told him that a complaint had been filed, a warrant issued, doctors subpoenaed, witnesses heard, and so forth, and the District Judge had made an order reciting so and so—something the Attorney General had set forth in his letter—and I said that I would attend to my business as County Attorney of Madison County, and if I needed any advice from the Attorney General, I would ask for it. I was surprised again: in due time I received a letter from Attorney General Haskell saying the papers in the case had been sent to him, and upon examining them he found them excellent; indeed, he had used them in preparing forms for use throughout the state.

My information is that Nahum Parker was not the name of the father. His name was Farnsworth. He had changed his name after leaving Illinois, why I do not know. But he was known as Nahum Parker all the time he lived in Madison County. After a time, George regained his reason and left Montana, going to Illinois to his relatives. He thereafter lived and died under the name of George Farnsworth. Some years after George was committed, Nahum Parker, taking the pistol with which his wife had been killed, went to the barn in back of his residence in Virginia City, and put a bullet in his brain.

A RICH MAN AND TAINTED BEEF

One of the first cases that came into the County Attorney's office during my tenure was a complaint against Alphonse Marion, a rich Canadian-Frenchman who lived at Laurin. The charge was selling big-jawed, or diseased, beef. It seems that this thrifty farmer, who was reportedly the richest man in the vicinity of Laurin except Jean Baptist Laurin himself, saw an animal suffering with actinomycosis, a disease which causes deterioration of the jaws and abscesses in the lungs, intestines, and other body parts, all of which could be transmitted to man. He proceeded to kill the animal, dress it out and sell a portion of it for beef. This was a crime, punishable by not more than a $500 fine or six months in jail, or both. Thinking the evidence sufficient to convict, I filed an information against Marion.

Marion promptly hired as his attorney my old nemesis, Will Clark, who was now back practicing law in Virginia City. Marion's other attorney was Robert B. Smith of Helena, who had been a candidate for Congress in the Fall of 1894, and who was elected Governor of Montana in 1896. I knew Bob Smith very well; he was one of the best trial lawyers I have known. I have tried cases with him and against him, and he has tried cases before me in the District Court and before the Supreme Court when I was a Commissioner.

But back to our story of Alphonse Marion and the tainted beef. During the month of May, 1895, I was busy preparing the case for trial. One of the incidents was that I went with my wife to Laurin and got the smelly head of the animal, which we took to Virginia City in the buggy which I had hired for the trip. The case came on for trial May 29. I had plenty of evidence as to the killing of the animal and the sale of some of the meat; also I produced the testimony of the State Veterinary Surgeon saying the animal was suffering from actinomycosis, which was dangerous to human life.

Then I made the mistake of letting the Veterinarian go home. Clark and Smith then put on the stand another of my old nemeses, Coroner McNulty, who testified that he had examined the head and all he found was necrosis. I hunted around and found my old friend Dr. Southmayd, who testified that necrosis was simply diseased bone, which was a necessary consequence of actinomycosis. The jury found Marion guilty and left the punishment to the court.

Clark and Smith announced that they were going to appeal the case to the Supreme Court on the ground that Judge Showers had given the jury an erroneous instruction. But Marion went to see his old friend, Henry S. Gilbert, asking him to see me and to say he would pay a fine of $500.00, and the costs of the suit (which were not taxable by law), if I could get the Judge to omit a jail sentence. Marion was terrified over the prospect of going to jail. I told Mr. Gilbert that I would submit the proposition to Judge Showers, which I did. He said very well, he would simply impose the fine. Marion paid the $500.00, to the disgust of his lawyers.

Just a word about the interesting man, Henry S. Gilbert, who pleaded on behalf of Alphonse Marion in this case. Gilbert was born in Pennsylvania and came west as a young man. He was a station keeper on the Overland Stage route under the famous (or infamous) Joseph Alfred Slade. Being in Salt Lake City, as I remember the story, he met and fell in love with a fine looking 16-year-old girl, of Mormon parentage. The young lovers agreed to elope and did so. The "avenging angels" were put on their trail, and the two were in imminent peril for a week, but they eventually reached the region over which Slade held sway and were safe.

Mr. and Mrs. Slade and Mr. and Mrs. Gilbert were great friends. When it was determined to go to Virginia City, each took some of the other's goods and chattels. Mr. Gilbert warned Slade that he must not behave as he had frequently when he had gone on a spree when he was superintendent on the Overland. Failure to follow that admonition led to Slade's execution by the Vigilantes in 1864, bringing to an end the life of a man who was excellent when sober but a madman when drunk.

Mr. Gilbert was a man with many friends; indeed he was liked by everyone. He was elected County Treasurer several times, and could have been elected to anything in Madison County. The Gilbert children came along rapidly, and there were eventually fifteen of them. Gilbert's friends joked him considerably over his large family and continuous increase. "Well," he said, "I consulted the doctor about it, and he told me I'd better get a bedroom away from the house, so I took some buffalo robes and slept in the brewery, and the next time Mrs. Gilbert had twins. So I went back to the house."

VINDICATION OF A FLEDGLING COUNTY ATTORNEY

After this victory over Clark and the astute Robert B. Smith, all with the undeniable help of the prolific Mr. Gilbert, I won my first case. In his six years in office, Will Clark had secured only one conviction in the District Court. I found the victory also gave me a real reputation in Madison County. The very next week, John B. Laurin retained me by the year. The retainer wasn't large, but it was something to be Laurin's lawyer. The case also brought me business from others.

One curious offer of business came from one of Marion's witnesses. I thought he was lying at the trial and told the jury so. He said Marion had promised to pay him $100 for his testimony but had paid him $25 only and wanted me to collect the other $75. I told the witness to forget that he ever spoke to me about it, that he had committed perjury and I thought so at the time; that a man could be sent to the penitentiary for perjury; to forget the whole thing and I would say nothing about it if he behaved himself from then on. Of course he would have denied his conversation with me and there was no other witness to prove the conversation than myself. But it made a good dog of him; I never heard of his doing anything else that was wrong.

I tried four murder cases in my four years, convicting all but one. In the four years I had but four acquittals, and I tried many criminal cases in Justice and District Courts. There were some unusual cases.

One was the outgrowth of the theft of some gold dust from A. W. Tanner of Red Bluff. Tanner had been mining on Pole Creek, which he thought was a bonanza, and had taken out some gold, which he had hidden in a porcelain chamber with a lid. He had hidden this and other articles in the attic of his store. A man named Q. Gilbert (not the exemplary family man already described) and another named McLean watched Tanner hiding the things and stole the gold dust. Now gold dust has its own peculiarities; one handling it can identify it; that is, he can tell whether it comes from Alder Gulch, or the Gravel range, or from Last Chance (Helena).

Shortly after the burglary, Gilbert and McLean took gold to the bank of W. A. Clark and Brother at Butte for sale. Alex Johnston, an experienced man, asked them where they got it, for the dust was not familiar to him. They said they had been mining out near Red Bluff. The bank bought it.

About four months later, Gilbert and McLean were displaying unusual amounts of money for them, and Tanner, who had missed his gold dust, became suspicious and began to investigate. He himself had dealt with the Clark bank for years. Talking with Johnston about it, that gentleman told of buying approximately the amount of gold dust Turner had lost, and described the appearance of the two men from whom he bought it. The general description fitted Gilbert and McLean. Johnston thought he would know them if he saw them again. Circumstances pointed at Gilbert and McLean.

I commenced a criminal action against them in Justice Court. Their arrest created a sensation in Red Bluff and vicinity. Gilbert was a man of good appearance, light complexioned, a little over average height, with a good face and a winning smile, a man who had many friends. McLean was a tall, light complexioned man, raw boned, not a man who inspired confidence by his appearance. On the preliminary hearing the two had brought many friends from Red Bluff and had, apparently, supplied them with money. These friends immediately set about cultivating sentiment for the accused.

We made the preliminary proof. My old adversary, Will Clark, who was defending, had his clients sit some distance apart in the body of the crowded courtroom. Johnston was called to the stand and qualified as a bank cashier familiar with the purchase of gold dust. He told of buying gold dust from two men, with particulars of the purchase. Asked if he thought he could identify the men if he should see them again, he answered in the affirmative, upon which I asked him to look over the courtroom and tell if he could see them.

He rose to his feet, looked over the group seated to the left of the center aisle, and said, pointing to Q. Gilbert, "There is one of them." I said, "Q. Gilbert, stand up." And when he did, I said to Johnston, "Are you sure that is one of the men?" and Johnston answered, "Yes, sir." He continued looking over the group where Gilbert was but shook his head; turning his eyes to the group on the right, he pointed to McLean, saying, "There's the other one." When McLean stood up, Johnston said, "Yes, sir, that's the man." The defendants were bound over to the District Court. Johnston was famous for his faculty of remembering names and faces. It was told of him that he remembered the face and name of every man who had dealt with him as cashier of the Clark Bank, and there were thousands of them.

In the District Court my recollection is that on the first trial, Gilbert was acquitted, and the jury disagreed as to McLean. They had demanded separate trials. On the second trial of McLean the jury again disagreed.

It was not long after this that I was faced with a new challenge: to run for reelection at a time when the entire country was in a silver panic and Republicans generally were denounced as "gold bugs."

10

RUNNING FOR A SECOND TERM AS COUNTY ATTORNEY

A Political Crisis Over Silver

Nominated For a Second Term

Weaknesses of the Primary System of Nomination

Skill at Cribbage an Aid to Campaigning

In 1896, a political situation developed which proved unsettling to Republicans in Montana. Nationally, the Republicans nominated William McKinley on a gold standard platform, virtually throwing silver in the ditch. At that time the prosperity of Montana depended upon the operation of its silver mines. The demonetization of silver had been a grievous blow. The silver mines were down, many miners thrown out of their jobs. The declaration of the Republicans was devastating.

Montana had voted for Benjamin Harrison for President in 1892 and elected John E. Rickards Governor, along with a Republican state ticket. Charley Hartman had been sent to Congress. The state had gone Republican in 1894, Hartman again being sent to Congress. It had two Republican Senators, Thomas H. Carter and Lee Mantle.

The Republicans were denounced as "goldbugs," and the name Republican was anathema to silver miners and those sympathetic to them. Then William Jennings Bryan, following his Cross of Gold speech, was nominated for President by the Democrats. Montana was wildly for him. Most of the Republicans were silver men who could not subscribe to many doctrines of the Democrats. Desiring to preserve their own party, they organized the Silver Republican Party, naming Charles S. Hartman for Congress, and placing county tickets in the field in most parts of Montana.

NOMINATED FOR A SECOND TERM

In Madison County, the Silver Republicans put up a full ticket, naming my old campaigning friend, Jake Albright, for Treasurer, Henry E. Steffens for County

Clerk, me for County Attorney, and Charles W. Mead for Surveyor. There were nominees for other officers, but after all these years, I do not remember them.

The Democrats put up a fine ticket, and most of the Populists went with them. In the state, the Democrats and Populists fused, nominating Robert B. Smith for Governor and A. E. Spriggs for Lieutenant Governor. Smith was posing as a Populist. The Republicans nominated O. F. Goddard for Congress and put up a fine state ticket. Colonel Wilbur Fisk Sanders threw his full strength to the Republican ticket.

Back in Madison County: Henry Steffens had been deputy under Barclay Jones, who had been County Clerk for many years. Barclay had been unbeatable. He died, leaving a wife and eleven children. Steffens was appointed to fill out his unexpired term and was serving when we nominated him for the office. Henry and I agreed to campaign together along the lines Jake Albright and I had followed in 1894.

The Democrats had nominated a strong man for County Clerk and had picked Montgomery W. Duncan of Pony for County Attorney. "Mont," as everyone called him, had been a miner; his brothers, and there were several, were miners. His father was a leading man at Pony, a member of the militant American Protective Association, and an ex-Confederate. All the former Union soldiers were for me, on account of my father, but I soon found all the ex-Confederates were for Mont, including my longtime friend, Gus Murphy. I would have bet on Gus, and was hurt to find him cool, whereas he had been hot for me in 1894. Long years after, in talking with Mont, I found out that his father, "Judge" Duncan, and Gus had been buddies in a Confederate regiment.

WEAKNESSES OF THE PRIMARY SYSTEM OF NOMINATION

I spoke of the nominations by Republicans, Silver

Republicans and Democrats. These were by the convention method, the "American way." It was by representatives selected by the people. The conventions tried to nominate the best men and to see that all sections of the county were represented by nominees. If the Democrats, for instance, nominated W. W. Morris for the Council (Senate in Montana then), the Republicans would say, "W. W. Morris is a mighty good man, and if we don't nominate one as good, Morris is sure to be elected." But under this abominable primary system, a Socialist device in my view, the nomination is by the mob, the people voting *en masse*, a sort of bastard "pure democracy," which the framers of the Constitution would have abhorred. A man nominates himself by filing a declaration of intention to run, or gets some people to sign a petition on his behalf, but as many can run as want to.

The primary was said to purify politics, to break up machines. It does nothing of the sort. It is corrupt, machine run, and easier to manage by the use of money than a convention ever was. Worse than that, the primary is the instrument of minority rule. It practically deprives the county districts of representation. Almost invariably, the nominees are selected from the county seat, if it is a big town, or from the biggest town if it is not. There was some "log-rolling" in conventions, of course, and doubtless money was used in Butte and other industrial centers. There is "log-rolling" under the primary system, too, and money is one of its principal factors.

SKILL AT CRIBBAGE AN AID TO CAMPAIGNING

Back to the campaign in Madison County in 1896: Henry Steffens and I took the Callaway family buggy and team. We campaigned from house to house. At Pony, where Mont Duncan lived, I found a decided change in attitude towards me. Even my friend and client, Major Isdell, was "off." I found a different attitude in mining camps.

Henry and I went from Pony to Sand Creek, a mining camp. Mont Duncan had worked there, as had some of his brothers. Henry was a fine billiard and pool player. At Sand Creek, he beat the "champion," winning the admiration of the boys there.

I could not play billiards or pool. While Henry was playing, I stood by a poker table and carelessly put my foot on the round of the chair of the player who was losing. Seeing what I was doing, he yelled, "For Christ's sake! Get your foot off my chair. You are bringing me bad luck!" After apologies, I moved away, going to a table where a game of cribbage was in progress. Here my knowledge gained from the old masters, Tom Robison and Serge McCoy, stood me in good stead. The two men playing "crib" were fighting for the championship of the camp, and the game was close. At the end I said, "You are both good players," but to the winner I added, "You wouldn't have won that game if your opponent hadn't overlooked a run." He said, "Maybe you would like a game," so I sat down and beat him easily. He said, "You are a better player than either of us."

Henry and I ran well in Sand Creek. At South Boulder we were among our friends. We were, however, approaching what we feared would be our crucial precinct—Gaylord, where one of the big mining companies was building a smelter on the banks of the Jefferson River. Three hundred men were employed, mostly strangers to our county. There weren't six old-time Republicans in the lot and it was doubtful whether they would vote for a silver man. The rest were for Bryan, but all were not registered. Any man who wasn't a Democrat was an object of suspicion—was he really for silver, or was he simply pretending to be?

Henry and I peddled our Webster cigars, $5.00 a box, and tried to be friendly. Having heard there was a decent man running a saloon and there was a billiard table at the place and the bosses, foreman, engineers and such spent their evenings there, Henry went to the saloon, made a good fellow of himself, and beat the champion at billiards.

In the bunkhouse thronged with men, a crowd was standing around a table at which two men were playing cribbage. Odd, I thought, when told it was for the championship. One player was a shrewd, taciturn man and the other a pleasant fellow who was playing a good game. Each had won a game and now they were playing the third. Finally the taciturn man won by a point. I said, "That game was well played by you both, but if your opponent had not overlooked a run of three, you would have lost by two points."

He looked up at me and snarled, "Well, you know so much about the game, maybe you'd like some of it." I replied, "I'll play you three games, best two out of three," and sat down. He was cocky, a good player. The cards ran pretty well and I beat him two games straight to the cheers of the onlookers, who pounded me on the back. They didn't like the taciturn and cocky man.

When I went back to the saloon, I found that Henry was winning his final game at billiards. Everyone was good natured and I met the principal men in the camp. Drank too much beer. Someone took us to a warehouse, got some mattresses and comforts, and made us a bed. In the morning, a little the worse for wear, we went on after breakfast, with good luck greetings. Henry and I led our ticket at Gaylord. He lost the camp by 16, I by 18, but our teammates lost it by 40 or 50.

We went to Waterloo, stopped with the Democratic warhorse, Pat Carney, who was friendly, but probably wouldn't vote for us, and on to Twin Bridges. The county fair was on. Henry, a good dancer, tried to dance with every girl there. He was not married and the girls liked him. Doubtless the girls were for him, but of course they couldn't vote. It would be almost two decades before they gained that privilege.

After Twin Bridges, we concluded to go to Silver Star. It was Democratic and had gone against me in 1894. It happened that a man had been accused of trifling with a woman in the vicinity and some people had tarred and feathered him and ridden him out of town on a rail. He and some friends wanted the culprits prosecuted. They had their eye on a man against whom suspicion was pretty strong. Someone swore out a complaint and the man was confined to jail. I did my best to get evidence, but those who knew the facts wouldn't talk. I was berated by residents of Silver Star because I "wouldn't do anything."

When Henry and I arrived at Silver Star, we went into a grocery store where a number of people had congregated. I knew they knew the facts about the tarring and feathering and that some of them were the ones who had been criticizing me. I told them I wanted the facts in the case, that I had no animosity against anyone but I wanted to do my duty as County Attorney. I said, "Some of you know all the facts; some of you were present when the affair was going on. Please tell me the facts." No one said anything. I then said, "I guess you are going to keep your mouths shut about the matter, but are going to keep on criticizing me. You are not good citizens; you can go to hell!" And I went out, slamming the door. After I left there was a silence, which someone broke by saying, "Well, that young feller's got some nerve. I believe he's all right." I got Henry and we left town at once.

I did not mention the election while we were in Silver Star, but I did better there than in 1894. My recollection is that the result in 1896 in Silver Star precinct was a tie. Twin Bridges looked all right, but I was a little apprehensive about Sheridan. Things looked better at Laurin than in 1894, and the upper Ruby did not worry me. Virginia City seemed safe.

This election presented a serious situation. If I did not win it, it would mean hard times. My civil business had been growing, but it had not yet developed into a real good practice. I had supported my father, mother and two brothers since January, 1895, and I was still doing so; I also had a wife and child. But, as I said to my mother, "I don't think all those prospectors and other poor people I've been helping in the last two years are going to fail me." That was a good guess. I carried Virginia City by a large majority. What they did to me in Pony was "plenty," but from around the county my majorities rolled up until my clear majority was 154. Pretty good, I thought, when I had to overcome 300 to start even.

Jake Albright and Henry Steffens did even better, but Charley Mead won by only four votes. All the Democrats, except those who ran against Jake, Henry, Charley and myself, were elected by considerable, some by large, majorities. Charley Hartman was elected to Congress, but the State Democratic ticket was elected in that politically divisive year of 1896.

11

SOME NOTABLE LEGAL CHALLENGES

John B. Laurin: Formidable Man and Client

A Challenging Probate and a Daunting Lady

The Boy Who Could Pick Locks

The Ennis Murder

Early in 1896, my client, John B. Laurin, died, and I attended his funeral. I had been at Catholic funerals before but never at a requiem high mass. Priests had come from Butte to conduct the funeral ceremonies, which were most elaborate. I had no religious prejudices whatever. I thought it was nobody's business what a man thought about religion, and I think so still.

It is appropriate here to tell something about the remarkable Mr. Laurin, however, for whom the town of Laurin was named. John Baptist Laurin came to Montana long before the discovery of gold in Alder Gulch. Legend said he was a foot racer among the Indians with whom he traded. His trading operations had covered a wide scope—from Fort Benton to Deer Lodge to Fort Bridger, and on the Upper Yellowstone.

Shortly after the discovery of gold at Alder Gulch, he established a trading store at a place then called Cicero, and began to acquire land. He raised horses and cattle on a large scale, and loaned money at high rates. He charged interest as high as two percent a month, perhaps higher, ten percent per annum on well secured real estate loans. The debtors made partial payment from time to time. He kept accounts and dates of payment in his head, and could usually tell, almost instantly, the balance due. He could neither read or write and of course couldn't figure on paper. He died worth over $150,000.00.

On his home ranch at Cicero, Laurin raised hundreds of chickens, usually employing a Chinese cook who looked after them. The chickens he sold; he would sell anything. A man told me of stopping to buy some chickens from him. Laurin told the Chinese what to do, but the Oriental was not too careful. In chasing the chickens, he pursued a pullet. Laurin yelled, "Non, non, not ketch ze poolet, ketch ze stud chickon!"

According to talk, Laurin had lived with the Indians, having wives as it suited him. After he settled at Cicero, he lived alone. Shortly thereafter a young woman, large of size, and comely in appearance, came with a wagon train from around Montreal, Canada. She came from St. Martin, she told me. Her maiden name was Adeline Legris, or LeGris. She could read with difficulty, could write a little.

Before starting from her home, she married a likable French-Canadian, and enjoyed his company until the wagon train was within what we now call Montana. The party camped on Sheep Creek, in present Beaverhead County, along the Salt Lake road. Her husband was shot and killed accidentally by one of the party. She had no choice but to continue; she was penniless and a widow.

Shortly after she arrived in Cicero, Mr. Laurin was told of her great misfortune by members of the party. He was sympathetic and kind. In a short time he told her of his life and situation and proposed marriage. It was really a business proposal; he thought it might be good for both of them. She thought, under the circumstances, that it was a good proposition and accepted. They were married and became fond of each other.

Laurin was beginning to grow heavy. In 1867 he weighed 250 pounds and his wife weighed about as much. He increased in size, but she did not. He was reported to weigh 400 pounds when I was a boy, and he was a sight, with his enormous paunch. Toward the end of his life, he began to lose weight, and at the time of his death, he was down to approximately 275 pounds. But he required an enormous coffin, and thereby hangs the tale.

The Catholic Church in Cicero, the town which had long since become known as Laurin, was a frame building, long enough to accommodate the members of the parish, but it had a narrow door. It was difficult enough to get the coffin into the church before the funeral, and it was yet more difficult for the pallbearers to take it out at the conclusion of the services, surrounded as they were by the huge crowd, and somewhat overawed by the solemnity of the occasion. Mrs. Laurin was much affected, and because the memory of getting the coffin from the church would not leave her, she resolved to change that condition.

The death of John Laurin was a virtual cataclysm to the town. He had been its founder, and, if one were chosen, undoubtedly would be its leading citizen. Among many people, he was an institution. They came to him for advice on many subjects; borrowed money; followed the course he indicated. He was a power in wielding public sentiment. I heard this story about the time Jack Edsall was running for Sheriff on the Republican ticket. The Republican Central Committee was having a meeting and from all reports it seemed that the entire Democratic ticket would be elected except, perhaps, the Sheriff. Andrew Jackson (Jack) Edsall had a good name and he was a fine man. There was a chance for him.

Someone at the meeting said, "Edsall will be elected if he can get a good vote at Laurin." Another said, "Well, I'm going to find out if he will." He left the room, got on his horse, and went to Laurin, twelve miles away. The next day he called some of the Committee together and announced, "Jack Edsall is going to be elected." "How do you know?"

"I went down to Laurin," was the reply, "and saw Jean Baptist in his store. We talked over both tickets. I said 'What do you think of Mr. Morris?' Old Laurin said, 'Beely Morris, he good man, everybody vote for him.' Then I said, 'I guess Henry Gilbert will be all right,' and he said, 'Henri, you bet.' Well, I found out he was for the whole Democratic ticket except for Sheriff. I asked him what he thought about Jack Edsall, and his face lighted up. He said, 'Jackee Edsall! By gar, he varra good man, he play one damn fine game pokair'!" Edsall was elected.

A CHALLENGING PROBATE AND A DAUNTING LADY

After Mr. Laurin was buried, Mrs. Laurin employed me to probate the will, and I gave the matter good attention. Along in August, 1896, I went to Helena on business. Sometime before that, I knew that Fred Cope, who had lived in Madison County, but who afterwards was a cashier of the First National Bank of Helena, had been in Madison County soliciting deposits. I knew the Laurin estate had a time deposit at that bank for $7,000.00, payable six months from date with interest at six percent per annum. I did not know much about banking, but I thought a bank that would pay six percent on deposits needed money pretty badly. While in Helena I met Will Thompson, my old playmate, who was an employee of Anton M. Holter, and in our conversation, I asked him what he thought of the First National Bank. He said, "I don't know anything about the bank, but I have no confidence in Erastus D. Edgerton, the manager." I said, "If you have no confidence in the manager you can't have much confidence in the bank." And he smiled.

When I got home I made a trip to Laurin, and while discussing business matters with Mrs. Laurin, I told her I got some information that led me to believe the First National Bank wasn't safe, and I wanted that $7,000.00 certificate to deposit in Henry Elling's bank in Virginia City. She objected, saying "that certificate it pays six dollars percent and we only have to wait two months to get cash and the interest."

I said, "You'd better get the $7,000.00 and pay no attention to the interest; if you don't, I'm going to report it to Judge Parker." "Well," she answered, "Maybe you know the best," and gave the certificate to me. I had her endorse it and offered it for deposit at the Elling Bank. Tom Duncan, the cashier, said, Elling being present, "you know you'll have to forfeit the interest," and I said I agreed, but advised him to give Mrs. Laurin credit for $7,000.00, which he did.

In about six weeks, the First National Bank, which had been Sam Hauser's pride and joy, failed to open its doors. Going down the street of Virginia City, Mr. Elling encountered me and said, "Lewie, you paid me a mean trick." Not thinking of the Laurin matter, I showed my astonishment, asking what I had done to him? He replied that I must have known something was wrong with that Helena bank or I wouldn't have deposited that certificate, and I ought to have told him, and now, by hell, he had lost the interest and he didn't know how much of the principal. I then told him of my conversation with Will Thompson and the reason why I had done as I did. I also told him I wasn't going to say anything against a going concern, it might be slander. He was a banker, I implied, and ought to have known what was going on.

When I told Mrs. Laurin all this, she was so pleased she gave me a quart of old port wine as an evidence—and it was strong evidence—of her appreciation. I closed the estate as soon as the year was up and received a good fee. I drew three wills for Mrs. Laurin, all the same, with slight changes. She was whimsical and would change her mind for small reason.

Here is an illustration: she had a young girl staying with her as a lady's maid and willed a legacy to her of $500.00. Going to Butte, she took the girl along. It was the girl's first visit to Butte and she was dazzled by what she saw. Going to a show with another girl, she left Mrs. Laurin alone for two or three hours and during that period, the old lady thought she wanted her maid, and the maid wasn't at hand. This so enraged Mrs. Laurin that she made a new will cutting out the legacy to the girl. I protested, tried to persuade her that the girl's behavior was one that might be expected in the circumstances, to scold her and forgive her. No sir, she would do nothing of the kind.

Mrs. Laurin was an intelligent woman, but after

figures reached a certain limit, she was lost. Like a man who doesn't know the difference between a million and a billion dollars! She knew the names and addresses of the persons she intended to make beneficiaries in her will, but she couldn't count above $6,500.00 to save her life. After she would give the names and amounts together with $10,000.00 for the church and charity, she would throw up her hands and say the money is all gone! I would say no, Mrs. Laurin, you have more than $125,000.00 to give away, and we would start all over again and come to the same result. This happened every time she made a will; same result.

She wanted a provision for a fine church in Laurin which would have a big door, so they could carry a casket out without trouble, and I would urge her to give $20,000.00 for the purpose. I would argue, "You and Mr. Laurin did not have any children; this town is your child; build a fine big church." "But," she would argue, "I want to give some money to the Catholic Orphans Home at Missoula!" "Give them $5,000.00; you can afford it," I would counter. "But I haven't got the money," were always her final words. It would come down to $8,000.00 for the church and $2,000.00 for the orphans in spite of all I could do.

I put a provision in the will bequeathing the legacy for the church to the Roman Catholic Bishop of the Diocese of Montana, requiring him to give a bond for an immediate construction of the church. He carried out the bequest faithfully, as was to be expected, and the town of Laurin has a fine stone church.

The deplorable thing to me was that Mrs. Laurin was leaving the residue of her estate to Fabien, her half brother in Kansas, and I figured Fabien would get away with $80,000.00 or more, and that's the way it fell out in the end. I wanted the bulk of the estate to remain in Montana, which produced it. She had erected a tombstone costing $2,500.00 at the grave of Mr. Laurin, and in her will expressed a wish to be buried by his side and had left money for masses to be said for the repose of his soul.

One day she sent for me and I drove down to see her. She wanted to know if everything "was fix" and I told her I thought so, why? The doctor had told her she must have an operation, she told me, and she was going to Montreal, and she wanted "everything fix;" she might not come back alive.

Naturally I pooh-poohed the idea, but she was serious. It was more serious than I even imagined. I said everything was all right so far as I knew, but did she have any gold? Apologetically, I said I knew how people in the early days when there were no banks got into a habit of saving gold, burying it. If she had done that and didn't come back, the gold would be lost or get into hands other than those she intended; if she had any, she had better put it in Mr. Elling's bank, which was safe.

She looked at me in silence, rose, went to the door, and called "Henri," and Henri Gagnon, her employee, came into the room. To him she said, "You stay here with Mr. Callaway." Then she closed the shutters on the windows of the dining room, in which we were seated, pulled down the curtains, closed both doors, the last one as she was leaving, and was absent for some time. She came in with two rotting buckskin bags which she placed on the table. One bag gave way and twenty dollar gold pieces rolled off the table and onto the floor. She said, "There should be $2,000.00." We counted and there was indeed that amount, all gold, nearly all in twenty dollar pieces with a few tens.

I laughed, and asked her where she had had that buried? She said, "Well, I guess no use to keep the secret now. Right where you'd never guess. Just where the servant put her foot every day. Just inside the door of the root house." If you've never carried gold in your pockets, you don't know how heavy it is. I put one bag in each pocket of my coat. It was dark, and I saw imaginary road agents all the way to Virginia City.

I was relieved when the gold was safely deposited in Elling's bank the next morning.

Now came the matter of probating Mrs. Laurin's will. At my suggestion she had made Frank H. Wilcomb, well known merchant and stockman at Laurin, her executor.

In the election of the fall before, my old nemesis, Will Clark, had been elected to the Legislature, a member of the House. Robert B. (Bob) Smith had been elected Governor. Of course every new Governor must do something and Smith, seeing that other states were doing it, recommended passing an inheritance tax law. The bill was entrusted to Clark, who having me and the Laurin estate in mind, inserted in the bill a section to the effect that no County Attorney nor any relative of the County by blood or marriage (this was to exclude me and my father) should act as attorney for an estate in anywise subject to the payment of an inheritance tax. I discovered this provision shortly after Mrs. Laurin died, and set about to make sure that Clark didn't get the estate. After I had a conference with Frank Wilcomb, he employed Julian Knight to handle it.

When the next large estate came along, that of Alex Metzel, my term as County Attorney had expired, and although Clark had been Mr. Metzel's attorney, the boys employed me. Incidentally, in a conversation with Governor Bob Smith, who was my friend, he told me that Clark had put in the "county attorney" provision without his knowledge. "I didn't know it was in the bill when I signed it," he told me.

THE BOY WHO COULD PICK LOCKS

During my second term as County Attorney, as in my first, it was frequently necessary for me to attend the justice courts. During my incumbency, in Union Township, in which Virginia City was located, we had, not at the same time, two exceptional men serving as

Justice of the Peace, Archibald McGown and Nathan D. Johnson. The latter was the smart and likable man we called Chunky whom we have already discussed.

McGown was an assayer, well educated, had been a Confederate soldier. He was a fair-minded man, naturally inclined to the right. In appearance he was tall and slender, straight as an arrow. I tried a good many cases before him, with a jury and without. I do not intend to load these memories with details of all of my lawsuits. But there was one which was unusual in character and the circumstances were extraordinary.

Old John Wall, who told of the alluvial deposits which he called the Apex, was peculiar, and he had a son, perhaps more peculiar. If the son had been well reared, not by an old prospector who lived alone, and had been given educational advantages, he might have been a genius. As it was, he had a mechanical turn which was unusual in a number of directions. In one direction, he had a flair for unlocking safes, picking locks, and stealthily prowling around in and out of places where he had no right to go, and he pursued this prowling proclivity both by day and night. Secretive, he did not talk of it, but it became known that he could unlock padlocks, safes and the like, which no one else in the little city seemed able to do.

A concern in town ran a saloon, keeping in a Diebold safe a considerable sum of money. One morning it was found that someone had taken something near $400.00 from it. The partner in charge was certain the safe was locked when he closed the saloon along toward midnight; but in the morning, the money was gone. The sheriff and police did not know what to do. There was no clue; actually, there wasn't any fact or circumstance which cast even a suspicion on a thief. Fingerprints were unknown in our town at that time.

Somebody was guilty, and reasoning that "somebody did it," and likely it was somebody who knew the conditions at the saloon, some officer arrested young Wall. It was upon the wildest suspicion. The boy had been in the saloon but seldom; he did not drink, smoke or play billiards. Likely he was then about eighteen years of age. Most boys of that age living in Virginia City had been in the saloon too often, but liquor was not sold to minors in that place.

The officer and the sheriff interrogated the boy, and there was no suspicion of third degree treatment. The boy's explanation of his whereabouts on the night of the "robbery," as the officers called it, did not ring true. He seemed frank enough about some things. Yes, he admitted, he could open the ordinary safe, could pick the ordinary lock. It was no trouble to go into any house in town; he thought he had been in every one in town, and usually at night. "But," he said, "I defy you to find I ever took or disturbed anything."

Judge McGown held a preliminary hearing. Old John had employed Will Clark to defend the boy. The showing made by the State was pretty slim. Clark moved for the prisoner's discharge. His Honor said, "The showing is not strong but I think it strong enough to call for an explanation; motion overruled." Clark made the mistake of calling the defendant to the stand. If he had not, I would have had to ask for a dismissal of the case.

But at the conclusion of the defendant's direct testimony I gave the boy a searching cross-examination. McGown permitted me to go over the ground, Clark objecting three times. During the cross-examination, an unusually strong earthquake occurred. The building swayed, and many people jumped from their seats. Wall, in the witness chair, sprang up. I said, "Take your seat, we'll go on after this earthquake quits." McGown, unexcited, said, "Though the Heavens fall, justice shall be done!"

Inside five minutes, Wall broke down and confessed his guilt. But he would not tell what he had done with the money. He said he hadn't spent a cent of it. John Wall was shocked; he believed the boy innocent. The officers had made a "thorough" search of John's cabin in Prospect Gulch, with no result. After John and the boy had been left alone, John told where the money was. The boy had hidden it in the looking glass which old John had over his wash basin for many years. The boy had removed the slender bits of wood which held the glass, placed the greenbacks behind the glass, and carefully replaced the wood. If the boy had not disclosed the hiding place, in all probability, the money might be there still.

THE ENNIS MURDER

During my second term as County Attorney, I encountered my most important murder case. Martin Peel, an old resident of the Madison Valley, sought out William Ennis on the main street of Virginia City and shot him. This was June 18, 1898. Mr. Ennis, one of the first three white men to settle in Madison County and the man for whom the town of Ennis was named, died of his wounds on July 4. It was a shocking tragedy.

The Ennis family employed Colonel W. F. Sanders to help me. Mr. Peel employed Walter Hartman, who took in Sam V. Stewart, a young lawyer whose name was to become well known in Montana. The defense was insanity, the contention being that Peel became insanely angry because of an unfounded rumor that Mr. Ennis had maligned him and sullied his character.

Colonel Sanders and I briefed the law on insanity thoroughly. The Colonel conducted masterful cross examinations of the defense experts' testimony and he and I prepared careful instructions to the jury. But Judge Parker had his own notions about insanity and gave an instruction that Sanders and I thought was wrong. I offered the argument and the Colonel closed it in a stirring oration. The jury found Peel guilty of murder in the first degree which then meant hanging. After my term expired, the Supreme Court reversed the case and sent it back for a new trial because of Judge Parker's instructions.

In the second trial, Mr. Peel was found guilty of murder in the second degree, and sentenced to fifteen years in the state prison. He died there. As I look back on this tragic case, I think the truth is that Martin Peel, an irascible man, probably was influenced by irresponsible gossip from people who should have known better. Some of this gossip cost the lives of two men, both old timers, who should have lived and died in peace.

12

LIFE AS MAYOR OF VIRGINIA CITY

The Birth of Jimmy and a Desperate Fight for Life
My Election as Mayor
How Not to Steal Gold
Another Important Client
A Busy Fraternal Life
Close Run For a Third Term
Birth of a Healthy Little Daughter
A Time for Politics

I decided in 1899 that I would not be a candidate for a third term as County Attorney. It was a great relief to be out of office, my own man. I was more exhilarated than I had been at any time since the previous May 1, when my father came in my office with the news that Commodore Dewey had sunk the Spanish fleet in Manila Bay. I was employed on almost every criminal case, on one side or the other, and was busy with my growing civil business.

In January, my old neighbor, Alex Metzel, died, and his sons, Frank and Albert, employed me as attorney for his large estate. In February, the Metzel brothers and I had to go to St. Paul on estate business. I was a little uneasy because Nell was "expecting." But I arrived home in good time.

Our son, James Edmund, named for my father, was born on March 6, 1899. Neither the baby, whom we called Jimmy, or his mother did very well from the first. My wife started to nurse Jimmy but was soon compelled to stop. She had contracted puerperal fever, and a battle ensued to save her life, which virtually hung by a thread for a good many days. The physician was Dr. Edgar A. Brooke, who had come to Virginia City some time before. When Nell's case became desperate, we called in Dr. Miller of Sheridan for consultation. Sheridan was twenty miles away and at that time the journey had to be by horse and buggy.

The disease dragged on. The fever was 104 every morning for several days, declining after Dr. Brooke gave a treatment, coming up next morning. But one morning the doctor didn't come. The fever raged at 104 all day and still the doctor didn't come. We thought he must have been called out of town, but his wife, who was quite distressed over the situation, did not know if he had.

I went everywhere I thought he might be, some not very reputable places, including McKeen's Saloon, where it was supposed gambling was carried on; I knew the doctor gambled occasionally. No one had seen him. About 6:00 in the evening, we were nearly frantic. Dinner was ready but no one had any appetite. I took a few swallows and went downtown again, to the doctor's office and all about, arriving at McKeen's Saloon a little before 7:00. No one had seen the doctor.

As I left the saloon, a man, afterwards a bootlegger whom I had earlier befriended, followed me out. Catching up with me, he asked, "Lew, how is your wife tonight?" "Pretty bad," I answered. "You're hunting the doctor, ain't you?" "Yes, I've looked everywhere for him." "Well," the man said, "I know where he is; he's down in McKeen's basement gambling; he's been there all night."

I went to my office, opened the safe and took out a cap and ball six-shooter which had been there for some time, and went back to McKeen's. I knew the bartender, and said to him without any preliminary talk, "I am going down into the basement, going to kick in the door, and I will kill any so- and-so who gets in my way. I'm going to get Brooke." "Hold on," he said, "I'll get him for you." And I said, "Be quick."

He went down the steps in a hurry, returning with the crestfallen doctor. I said to him, "You get to my house and get there quick." He asked no questions but went at once. He never knew how close death was to him that night.

After a while Nell began to improve slowly. She was little better than skin and bone. After convalescence commenced we used to give her alcohol baths. I could carry her from one room to another as I would a little child. Not until sixty days had passed after Jimmy's birth was Nell able to walk again.

MY ELECTION AS MAYOR

At last, with Nell's improving health, I was able to give full time to my law practice, and in 1900, I was elected Mayor of Virginia City. I started some reforms, but not many were needed. Among other things, the cemetery needed attention. The fence was not in good repair and the sagebrush grew at will among the graves. The King's Daughters had secured a water right, but the water was not being used. People had erected expensive monuments and had given some attention to individual graves. Cattle had got in and trampled all over the place. There was not a tree in the entire area. This sanctified spot, this resting place of so many excellent people, the scene of so many bitter tears, was disgraceful.

I got a small appropriation from the council, repaired the fence, and grubbed out the sagebrush. I set out two lines of trees from the entrance down to the Masonic part. Would you believe it, the Masonic trustees would not pay the small cost of furnishing trees, although I offered to water them free of cost. Not until the City trees were flourishing and beautifying the cemetery did a different board set out trees in the Masonic section. I went to the cemetery nearly every day to keep water on the young trees. When I couldn't go my father went in my place.

HOW NOT TO STEAL GOLD

I had not been out of the County Attorney's office long when my client Frederick R. Merk called me over the telephone from Silver Star. I had known Mr. Merk since I was a child. His was the first neighbor's house I remember being in. Our little house fronted on Broadway and his was on the corner of Idaho and Broadway. Both have been gone a long time. Mr. Merk wrote good English, loved the arts and music. He actually had a Steinway grand piano in his house in

Virginia City in those early days. He sent Ella, his daughter, to Vienna to study music when she was yet a young girl. He and his wife toured Europe. I remember their son William, or Willie, as a mean brat. He was some older than I was.

Mr. Merk was a man of some wealth, gained in mining. For a long time he had a mine above Silver Star. When I first knew it the name was the Broadway. The mine at different times produced a great deal of money. An ore chute would "pinch out" and the mine would be quiet for a time. Then through his own activity or through leasers, it would start again, and a new ore body would be found.

Some time before this, Mr. Merk had leased the property to the Glass Brothers, who operated it under the name of the Bowery Mining Company. Mr. Merk came to see me about the operations, bringing his correspondence. The Glass Brothers had employed McBride & McBride, of Butte. A heavy lawsuit resulted which I will not take the space to explain, but Mr. Merk won the suit, principally because he had all the correspondence. He had kept a copy of every letter he had written and had preserved all the letters he had received. The suit finally ended in the Montana Supreme Court, with Mr. Merk prevailing.

Then along came three men from Anaconda. Mr. Merk's telephone call was about them. Would I, he asked, see the County Attorney and Sheriff and come down at once? He told me a little—he could not tell me much safely over the telephone "party line." I saw County Attorney Mont Duncan and the Sheriff, telling them that I thought there was a good criminal case for them at the Merk mine. They agreed to cooperate in every way.

Taking a buggy, I drove the forty miles to Silver Star and thence up Cherry Creek about five miles to the Merk residence. It was an unusual residence for a mine. Mr. Merk had a piano, fine pictures on the walls, and good furniture. In fact, the house would have been a credit to an up-to-date Montana town of the period.

Mr. Merk told me his son, Willie, had gone to Helena, from which city he had telephoned, giving startling informaton. Willie was coming with photographs, and he might be home almost any minute. In the meantime, Mr. Merk told me this story: he had leased the mine some months ago to the men from Anaconda on a royalty basis. For a considerable time the mine yielded gold in good quantities, and the owner's royalties were substantial. Then they suddenly dropped approximately one half.

Observing the ore, Mr. Merk thought the grade was the same as it had been. He went through the mill and the assay office frequently and everything seemed normal. The gold seemed to be coming off the plates in copious quantities. The custom was to mould the refined product into bars. Two of these, less on the bottom than on top, were fitted together while still hot. Each was flat on bottom and top with sloping sides and ends. Two fitted together were hexagonal but bulging at the middle and ends. The practice was to ship the two bars, thus made into one, to the assay office at Helena, which shipped them as they were or melted them into ingots before shipping them to the mint.

Mr. Merk felt sure that some obscene dealing was going on: why had his royalties suddenly fallen to one half? He watched the cars of ore from the mine, the operation of the mill, the assay office, but could find nothing. Well understood by him, one of the Anacondans would take the bars in a black satchel to the railroad station and ship the bars by express to the assay office at Helena. Sometimes this was done by one partner, sometimes another. But usually the same man did it.

Within the week, Mr. Merk had gone into the assay office at the mine, in which he found no one but the assayer, who Mr. Merk believed was both discreet and honest. Mr. Merk asked, "How is the ore running?" to which the assayer said, "About the same." "Well, it has always run just about the same since you've been here, hasn't it?" "That's what the assays show." "Has the mill been saving the values?" Mr. Merk asked. "I think so, never heard any complaint," the assayer said. Then Mr. Merk explained his perplexity. "Strange," said the assayer, and went on with his work.

As Mr. Merk was about to leave, and as he neared a kind of work bench in the assay office, the assayer quietly remarked, "You might examine the cold chisel." Mr. Merk did so; it showed gold on its beveled edges. "What does this mean?" Mr. Merk asked. "Figure it out for yourself," the assayer said.

This man Merk was smart. Saying nothing further, he went home, thinking. Why did that chisel show gold? The "why" was plain enough: it had been used to split those bars in two. These halves were marketed separately; only one half was going to the mint. He told his discovery to Willie, who was smart, crafty and suspicious. Willie said, "Give me some money, I'm going to Helena."

First Willie stopped at the railroad station at Whitehall, where it was disclosed that one of the Anacondans had shipped so many bars to the assay office on certain dates. Willie took down the dates. In Helena, Willie found out that with the difference of a day or two, precisely the same number of similar bars arrived at the assay office from a bank in Anaconda. "Ah ha!" said Willie to himself, "one half the bars were sent from Whitehall and the other half from Anaconda."

While Willie was at the Helena office, a shipment came in from the Anaconda bank. The bars from Whitehall were still in the vault. The U.S. Assay Office man in charge had become interested when opening the Anaconda shipment in Willie's presence and the chisel marks were pointed out. Going into the vault, the assay officer brought out the bars lately shipped from Whitehall. Put together, the Anaconda and Whitehall bars fitted exactly, chisel marks and all. Willie asked if he might have photographs taken, and consent was granted. So Willie fairly flew to a photographer, who took pictures about 8x10 inches in size. One could see the chisel marks on the bars from Anaconda and Whitehall in the photos.

Willie, coming as fast as the trains and horses could bring him, reached the mine, his eyes snapping. He talked as he unwrapped the photos. He had been to the Anaconda bank at which one of the Anacondans carried an account. Yes, the bank had shipped parcels to the assay office in Helena at times. The bank would not give any further information. Willie thought he had enough.

Mr. Merk, Willie and I had a conference, in which we discussed these facts. The Merks thought No. 1 was the weaker of the three Anacondans; he had a wife and children and was a follower. No. 2, they thought, was a more decided character, but he would always listen to reason. But No. 3 was hard boiled.

I decided to confront the men after dinner. Placing the photographs on the piano in full sight, I asked Willie to bring in No. 1. When he arrived I explained that I was Mr. Merk's lawyer, and the reason for my presence, that I had come pursuant to an understanding with the County Attorney and Sheriff. I went on to say that Mr. Merk did not have any disposition to harm him, a man wth a wife and children, but that a crime had been committed. I suggested that perhaps he had had nothing to do with it actively, but he had profited by it. If it became necessary to arrest anyone, he would be included. I then explained to him the crime and as a clincher showed him the photographs. He said, "I told those damned fools they would get us into trouble and we were doing well enough by going straight." He knew all about it, and said he would tell everything he knew. We let him go with his promise that he would not mention our conversation to anyone or warn the others.

No. 2, as we anticipated, was more difficult, but I told him that we had information from the assay office at the mine all the way to the Government office in Helena, of the fact that half the gold had gone through an Anaconda bank, that No. 1 had confessed. We then showed him the photographs. He said, "I guess you got us; what do you want?" I said, "We want a cancellation of your lease, restoration of the money you have stolen. That means the three of you. If you do that we'll call it quits." He said he would do all he could, and we released him under pledge of silence.

Also as expected, No. 3 lived up to his reputation. He was indeed a hard case. He said he would do nothing, tell us nothing. We could go to hell. "No," I said, "you are the fellow that's going to hell." Then I told him the nature of the case we had against him, filling in blanks with my imagination, and showed him the photographs. "You go to hell," he said. "No, but I'll start you on the road to hell," I said savagely, and walked to the telephone. "Operator, give me the Sheriff in Virginia City." "Hold on," he said, "let's talk this over." "Talk nothing," I said, "unless you cancel this lease and make good what you have stolen, the Sheriff will be here before morning and he'll arrest you and your partners." "All right, I guess I'll have to do it." "Operator, please cancel that call."

That evening I drew up a cancellation of the lease that the three had signed, and got checks on the Anaconda bank for sums aggregating $5,000.00. The next morning Nos. 2 and 3 walked down Cherry Creek. That was the last the mine ever saw of them.

ANOTHER IMPORTANT CLIENT

In March 1900, busy in my office, I received a telegram from Levi G. Leiter of Chicago asking me to examine the title to some mining property and to come to

Chicago to advise upon it. I thought someone was playing a joke on me, and not until Joseph Smith, the telegraph operator, assured me the message was genuine, did I go to work. I examined the title to the main claims, got out an abstract on some others, and went to Chicago.

Mr. Leiter had reserved a room for me at the Sherman House. He had paid some money down to bind the bargain if the title proved good. My advice being that the title was good, Mr. Leiter gave me a check for $45,000 to conclude the deal. When some details were arranged, I took time to make a visit to my relatives in Tuscola, Illinois, and then arranged to go back home via Lincoln, Nebraska. My Uncle Ol, my mother's brother, lived in Lincoln, practicing medicine. I stopped a day in Lincoln with him and his wife and came on to Butte.

I remained Mr. Leiter's lawyer until I was appointed to the Supreme Court Commission.

A BUSY FRATERNAL LIFE

In 1898 I had joined with others in establishing Oro y Plata Lodge No. 390 Benevolent Protective Order of Elks in Virginia City, a decided accession to the city. Many of the best citizens of Madison County joined the lodge, and eventually it took in men from Beaverhead County. In the beginning I was Esquire, then Lecturing Knight, Loyal Knight, and Exalted Ruler. In 1900 I was Worshipful Master of Virginia City Lodge No. 1 A.F. & A.M., Commander of the Macabees, Worthy Patron of the Virginia City Chapter of Eastern Star, Exalted Ruler of the Elks, Mayor of the town, besides carrying on an active law practice. A pretty busy man.

CLOSE RUN FOR A THIRD TERM

I was re-elected Mayor in 1901. At the end of this term I wanted to quit and said so. To my considerable surprise, Joseph Smith II, a "stooge" of my old nemesis, Will Clark, came to one of my friends and dared me to run. Other Clark men said I was afraid to run. My friends told me I must not take the dare. The small group working for Clark, a rich man, told many who had supported me that I would not run again, and got them committed to Clark. My friends and I polled the town and concluded that while the election would be close, we could win. The situation was unpleasant; I wanted to quit but feeling was beginning to run pretty strong. So I decided to accept the challenge.

The campaign that resulted was a stem-winder. Clark and his group went into the saloons and spent considerable money. There are always enough fellows sitting on the fence to change an election. The night before election, I joined my friends, A. J. Bennett, Harry Steffens and Bert Vickers in campaigning the saloons. Men said to us, "Last night we drank with Clark, saying to ourselves we will vote for Callaway, and we will." My father had been quiet, but now he got into the fight with vigor.

Will Clark was so confident of victory that Mrs. Clark prepared a banquet supper for her husband and his lieutenants. The supper was not served, for at the end of the strenuous election day it was found that I had carried my own and Clark's ward and he had carried the ward in the lower part of the town. My majority was two votes, just as we had figured it.

BIRTH OF A HEALTHY LITTLE GIRL

On October 21, 1902, our second daughter was born. Named Frances Lathrop Callaway, she was always called Fan. She was a fine, fat baby, but she nearly starved to death. Her mother's mammary glands were lost during the severe sickness that followed Jimmy's birth, and she could not feed the little one. We bought all sorts of apparatus, then sterilized milk, baby foods and what have you, but the little girl was wasting away. Just at the right time, the Knight's cow had a calf, and her milk saved the day. Fan began to thrive and grow up to be a strong and healthy girl.

A TIME FOR POLITICS

When the political campaign of 1902 came on, I was again chairman of the Republican County Central Committee. I had played that same role in the disastrous political year of 1900, when Montana came into national disgrace because of political skulduggery. Let me tell you a little about that.

In 1889, William Andrews Clark of Butte had been elected U. S. Senator by the use of money; there is no doubt that bribing was practiced. This was a continuation of the Clark-Daly fight. Curiously enough, the public morals descended so low that for a time the bribery was condoned by the people generally, even encouraged by large numbers. The election was followed by a U.S. Senate investigation in which our Congressman, A. J. Campbell, took a leading part on the Daly side. Many witnesses testified, and Montana's shame was flaunted before the nation's eyes. One of our Democratic representatives confessed to receiving $5,000.00, which he said was for mining and legal expenses. He said he paid part of the money to me for investigations looking to the disbarment of my old enemy, Will A. Clark, then a Senator from Madison County. This was utterly false.

The next Spring I was invited to address the graduating class at Laurin. I had a large audience, and my speech was devoted largely to purity in private and public life. I denounced bribery and quoted liberally from the speech of Demosthenes on the crown. I thought I made a good speech but it didn't seem to make a dent. Political chicanery was not over.

Senator Clark resigned his seat before the Senate put him out. He came back to Montana for vindication, and got it in the election of 1900. It was said that some $40,000.00 came into Madison County. I believe it, but some of the money was kept personally by those who were to use it for campaign expenses. On the other side, money was spent but nothing like the million dollars spent by Senator Clark. Jesse B. Roote told me that he himself had checked out $90,000.00 as a disbursing agent for Senator Clark, and he didn't know "how much Charley Clark and the old Senator and others spent."

Money came to our committee from the State Central Committee, but we didn't know how to spend it; we were not trained in political corruption. For instance, after consultation with A. J. Bennett, I sent $50.00 to Alfred E. Lloyd, who kept a saloon at Laurin, telling him to use it for the election. He sent me back $32.00, saying he couldn't use it. Senator Clark was re-elected to the U.S. Senate, of course, and oddly enough, after all his shameful efforts to become a Senator, he never seemed to enjoy the work and Montana saw less and less of him after 1900.

As I said, I was chairman of the County Central Committee again in 1902, but this time we had no money. I wrote to Carl Swanstrum, who lived between the Big Hole and Beaverhead rivers, telling him we were broke, but we must see that the Republicans were registered. He wrote me saying he was glad we were broke; he didn't like this business of spending money in political campaigns. He would, he said, hitch up his horse and see that every Republican in his precinct "between the rivers" was registered.

That was characteristic of the Republican spirit that year. Many a time, in that campaign, I sat up thumping my typewriter until midnight. The result was that whereas the State Central Committee had furnished me a stenographer as well as money in

1900, we had elected but one man, Henry Steffens. In 1902, with none of the amenities, we licked the platter almost clean. The Democrats elected one man only in Madison County, Charley Hill for Sheriff.

My practice was increasing. My brother, Edmund, to whose education I had been contributing, was graduated from the University of Nebraska in 1902, and I took him into my office.

Then in March of 1903 came a turning point in my life. I was named to the new three-member Supreme Court Commission. That meant the beginning of my commitment of many years to the Montana judiciary.

13

LIFE AS A SUPREME COURT COMMISSIONER

A 35-Year-Old in Distinguished Company

Genial Friends and a Family Move to Helena

Encounter With Teddy Roosevelt

Working Ourselves Out of a Job

After the turn of the century, the Montana Supreme Court was hopelessly behind in its work, in large part because of the notorious copper wars. Strife in the courts between F. Augustus Heinze and the Amalgamated Copper Company and others had become so extensive and weighty that it was impossible for three Supreme Court Justices, no matter how able, to do the court's work and keep it anything like current. Indeed, in 1901 the court was about two years behind in its work, and by 1903 it was nearly three years in arrears.

An effort was made in 1900 to increase the court to five but it failed. In 1903 the Legislature was Republican, Governor J. K. Toole was a Democrat. All desired to increase the court, but the Legislature wanted to name the new members of the court and the Governor insisted that prerogative was his.

Finally, relief being imperative, a bill to create a Supreme Court Commission of three, the members to be selected by the court, was passed. The bill, not having been returned by the Governor to the House in which it originated within the time prescribed by the Constitution, became a law on February 23, 1903.

Section 1 provided in part as follows:

> "The Supreme Court of the State of Montana shall, on or before the first day of April, A.D. 1903, appoint three persons, of legal learning and personal worth, as commissioners of the Supreme Court. It shall be the duty of said commissioners, under such rules and regulations as said Court may adopt, to assist in the performance of its duties, and in the disposition of the numerous causes now pending in said Court undetermined.
>
> "The said commissioners shall hold office for the term of four years, from and after their appointment,

> during which time they shall not engage in the practice of the law. They shall each receive a salary of $4,000.00 per annum, payable at the same time and in the same manner as the salary of a judge of said Court.
>
> "Before entering upon the discharge of their duties they shall each take an oath to support the constitution of the United States, and the constitution of the State of Montana, and to faithfully discharge the duties of the office of commissioner of the Supreme Court, to the best of their ability. The said Court shall have power to remove any and all members of said commission at any time, and all vacancies in such commission shall be filled in like manner.
>
> "The term of office of said commissioners shall expire at the end of four years from date of their appointment, and no further appointments shall be made, but this act shall thereafter be inoperative."

It was not difficult to select three persons "of legal learning and personal worth." The difficulty was to select three competent lawyers who were wholly independent and who were not allied with the respective contenders in the lawsuits which were overwhelming the court. It was agreed by the justices that the commissioners should be satisfactory to all the justices. I am told there was a great scramble for the positions. I believe none of the three selected was an applicant. For myself, the first I knew (except that I knew the bill has been introduced and hoped it would pass) was when Jacob Albright, Senator from Madison County, telephoned me saying he had been asked to ascertain if I would take the appointment if offered.

At 35 years of age, I was the youngest of the three chosen. The others were two distinguished lawyers, John B. Clayberg of Helena, and William Henry Poorman of Kalispell.

I left Virginia City on the stage on March 30, 1903, going to Twin Bridges, Whitehall and Logan, reaching Helena that night. For a few days I was the guest of Chief Justice and Mrs. Brantly.

On April 1, 1903, Judges Clayberg, Poorman and I were sworn in in the courtroom of the Supreme Court in the Capitol and took our seats. The Justices sat on their bench and we in chairs immediately in front. (I wondered if this was an April Fool joke on the people of Montana).

Our duties were not exactly clear in the beginning. Judge Milburn thought we should write opinions as clerks for the members of the court. Knowing the California system under which the commissioners' opinions appeared under their own names, the approval of the court following, I said to Judge Brantly that if my opinions did not appear under my name I would resign and resume my practice. And I knew Clayberg and Poorman felt the same way, whether or not they said so. That policy was adopted.

My first opinion, Lees v. City of Butte, 28 Mont. 27, was printed in both series of the select cases published for national distribution, in the American State Reports and Lawyers Reports Annotated. Others of my opinions were chosen by one or the other of those publications. The work was hard but not very confining.

GENIAL FRIENDS AND A FAMILY MOVE TO HELENA

When I first went to Helena to work with the court, after staying a week with the Brantlys, I engaged room and board with Miss Dundas at 59-61 Park Avenue. Regular roomers there were E. W. Beattie, Surveyor General (the General); his brother (the Major); Major Hosfeld, superintendent of the Federal Building then in the course of construction; William F. Scott, state game warden; E. L. Abrams, newspaper solicitor; and H. J. Goodale, federal employee. A regular boarder was W. J. Cooke, and Hon. Hiram Knowles, Federal Judge, boarded with Miss Dundas when he was in Helena.

This was an interesting group. General Beattie was

a genial man, a politician of sorts, Senator Carter's right hand. All were interesting. I had known Judge Knowles by reputation since the 1870s, knew of him and his work since some time in the 1880s. He and my father were members of the Constitutional Convention of 1869. The Judge and I became good friends. We used to sit on Miss Dundas' back stoop after dinner and talk the summer evenings away.

After the summer vacation was over, I sublet Judge Milburn's furnished residence in Lenox in order for my family to join me. There was a group of fine houses in Lenox, occupied by fine people. Our neighbors were the Keatings, Claybergs, Holloways, Howrys, Bradshaws, Kleinschmidts, Rochesters, Holmes, Knowles, Barbours and Calderheads.

It was a fine place for children and there were many living in Lenox. We had Miriam, Jimmy and Fannie, and Emma, Nell's sister, came from White Sulphur Springs and went to high school. She was an attractive girl, popular with the young people, and we got to know many of them. Our neighbors gave dinners to which Nell and I were invited and we had many good times.

My mother and father separately visited us at various times. They did not come together; one had to stay in Virginia City. My brother, George, was at Ann Arbor at the time. He went to school at Tuscola, Illinois, and later the University at Ann Arbor. George's experience at the latter school gave me cause to reminisce. When I was at Ann Arbor, the "frats" wouldn't look at me. I was too poor. But when I was appointed Supreme Court Commissioner, the fraternities at Ann Arbor wanted George right off. George wrote me saying the Phi Delta Gammas wanted him, and as I had let Edmund join them at Lincoln, wouldn't I let him? Of course I did.

Uncle John Woodson came to visit us at Lenox. We enjoyed his visits. Altogether, we look upon our life at Lenox with satisfaction.

ENCOUNTER WITH TEDDY ROOSEVELT

In April, 1903, it was announced that the Grand Lodge A.F. & A.M. would lay the cornerstone of the Arch at the Gardiner entrance to Yellowstone National Park. Frank E. Smith of Lewistown was then Grand Master, H. S. Hepner of Helena, my classmate at Ann Arbor, was Deputy Grand Master, and I was Senior Grand Warden. The four principal officers wore silk hats.

The Masons chartered a special train, and many notable Masonic figures went along, among them Judge Brantly, Past Grand Master. The voyage was enjoyable; there was a good deal of fun en route. President Theodore Roosevelt was to be there. Upon arrival at Gardiner, the Grand Lodge assembled about the stone awaiting the great man. He came on horseback with an escort of soldiers, all mounted.

We went through the ceremony, the President spreading the cement, after which he delivered an address from a stand built nearby. Then he held a reception in his private car, there waiting. Many of us met and chatted with him. I had been told that he had a marvelous faculty of remembering people: if he met a man he would remember him for years. Maybe that was so in some cases. But the following May he came to Butte, and he did not recognize me.

The famous Copper War was on in all its intensity and the fighters were striving for advantage. At the time, F. Augustus Heinze controlled Mayor Mullins of Butte. The Mayor gave a large dinner at the Thornton Hotel in Butte to which many prominent men were invited, among them the members of the Supreme Court and the Commissioners. There was a special train from Helena, and Judge Brantly and I went. The President spoke from a balcony built from the second floor of the Finlen Hotel. Prior to the speaking, many were introduced to "Teddy," I being one. He had completely forgotten me. Judge Brantly thought the great man had forgotten him as well. When Judge Brantly said to the President, "You met Mr. Callaway at Gardiner," the gentleman said, "Oh, yes," but I am sure he didn't remember that I was at the cornerstone laying and that I had had one of the principal parts.

Mayor Mullins introduced the President to the great crowd at the intersection of Arizona and Broadway. Becoming oratorical, the Mayor said this was the great soldier who "led the charge up San Diego hill." The President said, "Mr. Mayor, you are heaping new honors upon me!"

The dinner at the Thornton was a grand affair. The dining room walls were covered with orange blossoms imported from California; the table in the shape of a horseshoe glittered with silver and wine glasses.

The Mayor presided, the President on his right, and next to the President was Chief Justice Brantly. (Mr. Heinze was then anxious to have Judge Brantly appointed federal judge). Across the table inside the horseshoe was Seth Bullock, whom the President had known in his Medora ranch days. Senator Clark was seventh man from Mayor Mullins on his left and I was next to Senator Clark. There was a cocktail at each plate, followed by much champagne. Elegantly clad waiters poured champagne from quart bottles as soon as one drained his glass. The food was excellent. While not impolite, the President spent most of his time, not in conversation with the Chief Justice, but in recounting experiences with Seth Bullock.

The crowd grew noisy with champagne, and after the dinner broke up, Senator Clark went into the barroom, climbed upon the bar, and sang the Star Spangled Banner, which legend said he never did unless intoxicated. As nearly as I could tell all, with a few exceptions, were pretty high. The President was to address the miners at Columbia Gardens, and some feared he would be unable to deliver his speech because of too much drink, but the evening was cool and the ride was beneficial. Those who heard the speech said the President fairly outdid himself.

Years later, in 1912, Mr. Roosevelt sued a newspaper publisher in Michigan for saying that he, the Bull Moose candidate for President, had drunk to excess. At the trial, Mr. Roosevelt said, according to the newspaper report, that he never drank anything but champagne and that sparingly. I said to Judge Brantly, "Why I saw him drink that cocktail at the Heinze banquet," and the Judge said, "Yes, and he ate the cherry!"

I still have the menu given to the guests at that banquet. It was a thin copper plate with the list of eatables and drinkables stamped thereon, with a silver pendant attached. It was said those menus cost $11.00 each.

WORKING OURSELVES OUT OF A JOB

When court adjourned in 1904, we Commissioners were aware that we had nearly worked ourselves out of a job. Three years behind when we took office, the court was by now nearly current with its work. It was a signal to me to look at other possibilities, including Judge of the Fifth Judicial District.

Writing this after the close of my entire judicial service and looking back, I conclude without reservation that my district judgeship, which we deal with in the next chapter, was the most satisfactory. It is true that I enjoyed my work as Supreme Court Commissioner but there was the consciousness ever present that I was a subordinate not allowed to follow my personal inclination if it differed from the will of my superiors.

I did not say anything in my opinions which I thought was not the law, but at times I followed a stricter interpretation than I would have had I been allowed free expression. The experience of being a Supreme Court Commissioner, being regarded by the people generally as a member of the Supreme Court, after twelve years as a country lawyer and during the Copper Wars, was flattering to the vanity, I will admit. Except for an occasional superciliousness on the part of two of our superiors, which I now think was unintended, all treated us with consideration and respect. This means the state officers, capitol employees, the lawyers and the people of Montana. One felt that he was in a small measure making the local history of his times.

But now it was time to leave the Supreme Court as a Commissioner and seek out the district judgeship which was to engross me for the next eight years.

14

ON BECOMING A DISTRICT JUDGE

The Decision to Run

The Nomination and a Hard Campaign

A Full Legal Calendar

A Second Callaway Son is Born

My Colleague Joseph Poindexter

In 1900, the Republicans had insisted that I run against Judge Mongomery H. Parker of the Fifth Judicial District, but I would not do so. Again in 1904 they began urging me to run. Sure my term as Supreme Court Commissioner would be cut off no later than April 1, 1905, although we had been appointed for four years, I finally determined to make the race. This decision was communicated to the Republicans in Beaverhead, Jefferson and Madison Counties, which comprised the Fifth Judicial District. I was informed I would be nominated without opposition.

But now another situation arose. F. Augustus Heinze, who had been so eager to have Judge Brantly made federal judge, now wanted to defeat him. This was undoubtedly because Judge Brantly, who just would follow the law and do right as nearly as he could, had written opinions and concurred in others against the Heinze interests. Judge Brantly had wanted to quit and had put out feelers looking to a connection in private practice, but no definite conclusion had been reached.

Convention time inexorably came on and Judge Brantly felt himself under fire. The convention was in a wool warehouse in Billings. Judge Brantly had gone to Deer Lodge to attend the funeral of Captain James H. Mills. As soon as I arrived in Butte on my way to the convention, Carlos Warfield, John McGinnis and other Heinze men literally pursued me, saying Judge Brantly did not want to run, wanted to find a graceful way out, and so forth, and they wanted to nominate me for Chief Justice. On the train there was a boom on for Callaway for Chief Justice. I told them I was committed to Judge Brantly and would not run. Nevertheless they kept at me and at my friends.

The Heinze men said if I would not run they would find someone else. As soon as I reached Billings, I telegraphed Judge Brantly urging him to come to Billings, which he did. I took him to lunch and told him the whole story, advising him to get busy with his friends; that I did not believe Heinze could defeat him, but not to take any chances. I got the Madison County delegation together and we passed a resolution to vote as a unit, and another to support Theodore Brantly for Chief Justice. We all wore ribbons bearing the legend 23 as 1.

The Heinzes prevailed upon Colonel W. F. Sanders, an enemy of the Court, to seek the nomination for Chief Justice, and did their upmost, but Judge Brantly was nominated easily. James J. Page, a member of the Madison County delegation, wanted to vote for Sanders and asked us to release him, but we declined to do so and cast 23 votes for Theodore Brantly.

THE NOMINATION AND A HARD CAMPAIGN

I was nominated for District Judge. I had found in the campaign of 1902 that Heinze had strength in the Fifth District. Now I found that by reason of his reduction plant at Basin he controlled Jefferson County. Always having been in doubt of his sincerity, believing he simply wanted to use me, I set about to find out whether he intended to support me for District Judge. If he were consistent, wanting me to be Chief Justice, he would support me for District Judge. He and his men pretended to be friendly, but I could not find any evidence of it in Jefferson County. His head man at Basin was W. A. Kidney. He was inclined to be friendly and was a square man.

In my campaign in Jefferson County, I went to Basin and sought an interview with Kidney. I said to him that I was not soliciting his support. I would be glad to have it, of course, but I knew he was obligated to follow the wishes of Mr. Heinze. I simply wanted the truth: was Mr. Heinze intending to throw his strength to me or not? Mr. Kidney said, "I am sure Mr. Heinze has nothing against you personally, but it happens that your name appears on the ballot ahead of the legislative candidates, and we have orders to vote the Democratic ticket straight from the top down including the legislature. On county offices the men can do as they please." I thanked him, and set out to get votes elsewhere. I figured I would lose Basin by 200 votes and Boulder, Judge Parker's hometown, almost solidly, which would be about 200 more. Yet in the final count my memory is that I lost Jefferson County by only 22.

Beaverhead County was Republican and I had some friends there, some of whom I had ridden the range with, but Judge Parker, who had held the office since 1896, had been popular in that county. I found that he had some strong supporters. The Democrats were generally for him. At Bannack I met Fielding L. Graves who had been with my father in the Constitutional Convention of 1889. He said, "You've got a hard man to beat," and I said, "So has he." My friends had fun spreading this story. Even my friend Alf Decker said, in horse racing parlance, "I'm afraid Parker has the pole."

I campaigned the county thoroughly, carried every precinct I visited, and lost everyone I did not visit except Argenta, where my old White Sulphur Springs friend Marcellus Pyle turned the trick for me.

I must relate an unusual experience. John S. Baker, candidate for County Clerk, a former resident of Lima and popular there, took me with him to that place to campaign.

The year before I went to work with the Supreme Court, I was employed to assist Mont Duncan in the prosecution of one John White—Jack White as he was generally known. He was accused of horse stealing. It was said he stole a herd of horses, taking them from Madison County into Beaverhead. The fact was that he and some boys in his employ had stolen a few horses from the upper Ruby Valley, driving them up Sage Creek, over onto the Sweetwater range and down into Beaverhead Valley. I knew the country thoroughly, having ridden over it many times. I knew the range, the trails running through it, and the cut-offs that experienced range riders used. The State made a good case. The defendant sought to prove an alibi devised by W. S. Barbour of Dillon, a noted criminal lawyer. He was good at alibis.

I cross-examined the defense witnesses. It developed that they, under Jack White's leadership, had been in Madison County for Jack's horses, so they said. Having but slight knowledge of the country, they soon were in trouble over their route. They were separated so they did not hear each other testify. One, a bright boy, was a nephew of one of my special friends. I soon had him "spitting cotton." He didn't know where he had been. Rising from my seat I went close to the witness stand and said, "Now, I am not trying to confuse you; I simply want the truth. You are under oath. Just tell the truth as you yourself remember it, and we'll get along first rate." He did just that with the result that he confessed that he had been telling what he had been told to tell. He went on to say that he knew they were out to steal horses, that he knew the horses were stolen, that Jack White told them the horses were stolen.

The jury found Jack guilty, and he went to Deer Lodge for a year. He was furious at me, saying when he got out he would beat me to death, "stomp" me into the earth. Physically he was able to do just that. He was over six feet and powerful, with a mean disposition. I was used to threats, heard these and forgot them.

Now back to the campaign for District Judge. After having covered Lima pretty thoroughly, John Baker said he had some private business to attend to and he would have to leave me. "There's a saloon at the end of this street, the last house; I guess you can handle that yourself." So I went to the saloon at the end of the street. The front door was open, no one inside but an old "stew bum" asleep in the rear, and the tall bartender. The bartender was Jack White.

I was scared, instantly having visions of the ex-convict coming over the bar to beat me to death. I knew if I ran, and I wanted to run, he would overtake me in a dozen jumps and start on his devilish work. There was but one safe thing to do, and I did it: I walked to the bar holding out my right hand and said, "Hello, Jack, I haven't seen you since we were in court at Virginia City. Didn't I give you a good skinnin?" He said, "You little red headed s.o.b., you sure did. Have a drink." We drank, talked amicably, and he promised to do all he could for me. I carried Lima by a large majority.

My majority in Madison County was large. The day after election I telegraphed my wife who had gone to White Sulphur Springs from Virginia City to remain until after the election, that I had been elected by 300 votes. It turned out to be more than that.

Nell and Fannie came to Helena on Thanksgiving Day to the Grandon, at which hotel I had engaged rooms until sometime in December. I worked with the Supreme Court until December 15 and about that time resigned, taking my oath as Judge of the Fifth Judicial District before Governor Toole. Purchasing some furniture, we went to Virginia City again, reaching that town on December 18. We took the Leinen Weber house on Cover Street looking south to the courthouse.

A FULL LEGAL CALENDAR

After my first term began, I had to work hard with congested calendars. My salary was only $3,500.00, and I had to pay my own expenses. I had a bed placed in my chambers at Boulder and at Dillon, boarding at a hotel. In Dillon from the beginning I was invited to dinner at the homes of the leading families.

In the beginning it was not so at Boulder, which was resentful over losing the Judge of the District. That feeling soon passed away as my tenure continued. George Pfaff, clerk in my first term and his wife entertained me, as did George F. Cowan and his wife, and Dr. and Mrs. Leighton were always my friends. In my second term William T. Sweet and family were gracious, and many others in Boulder as well.

A SECOND CALLAWAY SON IS BORN

On September 12, 1907, Llewellyn L. Callaway, Jr., a fine healthy boy, our fourth child and second son, was born. The September weather was fine and bright and colder than usual. The new baby was soon bundled up and enjoying, we supposed, the fine cool air on the porch of the newly constructed little white house on the hill in Virginia City. The nurse, a young Irish girl, was quite inexperienced and paid little attention to the new baby or the increasingly cold weather. Result, a member of the family checking on the baby found him blue with cold. Soon all the women in the neighborhood were taking turns holding the cold child in the hot oven of the wood-fed stove. It was a tough ordeal for the women, who worked at this life-saving task for hours. Finally the little boy showed signs of recovery. After this rude start he grew up to be an active and happy little youngster. It was a dramatic start for the little fellow who was first known by the nickname U.U., which later evolved into Pete.

MY COLLEAGUE JOSEPH POINDEXTER

Work was increasing in my district, and I was helping other judges. The Milwaukee Railroad building through Jefferson County made additional business. Edwin Norris, who had been Lieutenant Governor, was elected

Governor in 1908. He and I being friends and viewing the situation confidentially, thought the Fifth District should have two judges. The governor agreed that if we could induce the Legislature to provide the additional judge, he would appoint Joseph B. Poindexter of Dillon. I drew a bill to that effect and upon its passage, Governor Norris appointed Mr. Poindexter. He was an excellent selection and made a fine judge. My recollection is that Poindexter was appointed my coadjutor in the Fifth District in 1909. We got along famously, ran the business of the District as if we were law partners.

In 1914, I think it was, Governor Stewart appointed him Attorney General, Dan Kelly having resigned that post to enter the employ of the Anaconda Company. Attorney General Poindexter served through 1916, when Sam C. Ford, later Governor, succeeded him by election. President Wilson appointed Judge Poindexter to the post of Associate Justice of the Territory of Hawaii, and after his term expired he practiced law in Honolulu. President Franklin Roosevelt appointed him Governor of Hawaii, and re-appointed him. Judge Poindexter was serving as such when the Japanese attacked Pearl Harbor on December 7, 1941.

The James E. Callaway home in Virginia City, with Mrs. Callaway standing with a child in front of the gate. Others in the picture cannot be identified.

Hunting trip, Lew Callaway in middle, right side

Mary Elizabeth Link Callaway in her later years

Montana Historical Society Photograph Archives

Helena, looking south from Sixth and Main, 1928

The Callaway home at 1400 Third Ave. No., Great Falls. The high school building with spire can be seen in the background. The three oldest Callaway children, Miriam, James and Frances, all attended classes or graduated from there.

Montana Historical Society Photograph Archives

Great Falls, circa 1920, looking south on Third Street

Judge and Mrs. Callaway at home in Helena, ca. 1940

The Callaway home at 427 West Lawrence in Helena

Judge Llewellyn L. Callaway
portrait by Jack Beauchamp

CHARLES NELSON PRAY
(1868–1963)

Judge Callaway's law partner in Great Falls, 1914–1922. A native of Potsdam, N.Y., Judge Pray graduated from the Chicago College of Law and, upon admittance to the bar in 1892, opened his practice in Fort Benton, Montana. He was elected to the U.S. Congress in 1907 and served until 1913. He was appointed judge of the U.S. District Court of Montana in 1924 and served until his retirement in 1957.

Montana Historical Society Photograph Archives

JOSEPH MOORE DIXON
(1867–1934)

As Montana Governor, he appointed Judge Callaway in 1922 to fill out the unexpired term of Chief Justice Theodore Brantly. Born in North Carolina, Governor Dixon was educated in Indiana, North Carolina and Missoula, Montana. Served as prosecuting attorney of Missoula County, elected a member of the Montana House of Representatives in 1900. Elected to the U.S. House of Representatives and served from 1903 to 1907. Elected to U.S. Senate and served from 1907 to 1913. Elected Governor of Montana in 1921, serving until 1925. Remaining years were spent as Assistant Secretary of the Interior.

Montana Historical Society Photograph Archives

SAMUEL VERNON STEWART
(1872–1939)

A long-time professional and personal friend of the Callaways beginning in 1893, when both Lew Callaway and Stewart practiced law in Virginia City. Educated in Kansas, he opened his law practice in Virginia City, serving as city attorney for five years and as Madison County Attorney for two terms. Served two terms (1913–1921) as Governor of Montana. Later practiced law in Helena amd was appointed to the Montana Supreme Court in 1933. He was serving out his second term on the high court when he died in 1939.

Montana Historical Society Photograph Archives

THEODORE BRANTLY
(1851–1922)

Married to Lew Callaway's cousin, Lois, Theodore Brantly was a close professional and personal colleague. He is considered by many to be one of the finest judges ever to serve on the Supreme Court of Montana. Born in Tennessee, he was educated in that state, including a law degree earned at Cumberland University in 1881. He practiced law in Tennessee until 1883, when he migrated westward, arriving in Deer Lodge, Montana, in 1887. Elected to the Third Judicial District Court bench in 1892, his well-reasoned opinions soon made him known throughout the state. He was reelected a district judge in 1896 and, in 1899, was elevated to the Supreme Court. He served as Chief Justice for nearly a quarter century until ill health forced his retirement in 1922.

THE CHILDREN OF JUDGE AND MRS. LEW CALLAWAY

JAMES EDMUND CALLAWAY
1899–1946

MIRIAM (MIMI) CALLAWAY
1896–1981

FRANCES LATHROP (FAN) CALLAWAY
1902–1934

LLEWWLLYN LINK (PETE) CALLAWAY
b. 1907

MARY ELIZABETH CALLAWAY
b. 1917

THE CHILDREN OF JUDGE AND MRS. CALLAWAY

MIRIAM (MIMI) CALLAWAY, born July 6, 1896, Virginia City, Montana. First child of Lew and Nell Callaway. Very bright, attended Wheaton College, Massachusetts, after graduating from Great Falls, Montana, High School. In 1919 married William Harper Jones, just returned from serving with the U.S. Army in France in World War I. They had two sons, now Dr. Harper L. Jones and Dr. Llewellyn L. Jones. Her husband died in 1934. In 1940, she married Sam D. Goza, Jr., a well-known Helena, Montana, attorney. Miriam died in Helena in 1981.

JAMES EDMUND (JIM) CALLAWAY, born March 6, 1899, Virginia City, Montana. Graduate of Great Falls High School, then spent a year at Staunton Military Academy in Virginia. When the U.S. entered World War I, he joined the Navy, serving as a gun-pointer on the U.S.S. Alabama. An accomplished horseman, hunter and fisherman, Jim loved the out-of-doors. He lost his life in a blizzard in the Lincoln country in 1946 when he went to help some stranded hunters.

FRANCES LATHROP (FAN) CALLAWAY, born October 21, 1902, Virginia City, Montana. She was bright, vivacious, pretty and popular with both men and women. After Great Falls High School, she attended Mills College, California, and the University of Montana, Missoula. In 1932 she married Sam D. Goza, Jr., a Helena attorney. A son, Samuel Dupuy Goza III, was born to this union. He grew up to be a successful medical doctor, practicing in Fresno, California. To the great sorrow of her family and host of friends, Fan was killed in an automobile accident in August, 1934.

LLEWELLYN LINK (PETE) CALLAWAY, JR., born September 12, 1907, Virginia City, Montana. Graduate of Helena High School, 1926. Graduate of Dartmouth College, 1930, with a B.A. degree. Earned M.B.A. from Harvard Business School, 1932. Spent five years with The Condé Nast Publications, 1932–37. There followed 25 years with Time. Inc., 1937–1962. (War service: Lt. U.S.N.R., War Production Board 1945.) Publisher of *Newsweek*, 1963–1969, Vice Chairman of *Newsweek*, 1969–1972. Married Helene A. Callaway of Denver in 1936. The two children of this union are Peter A. Callaway of Santa Fe, New Mexico, and Elizabeth Woodson Callaway, an attorney of Oakland, California.

MARY ELIZABETH CALLAWAY, born March 22, 1917, Great Falls, Montana. Graduate of Helena High School and attended Northwestern University. Married Dr. Gordon L. Doering September 14, 1939. Children: Charles, Jean Randolph, Bruce Callaway, Mary Ellen and Thomas. Mary is very bright and attractive to men and women, a very popular girl and woman. She is and has been the darling of her family. She continues to make her summer home in Helena and winters in Palm Desert, California.

15

EXPERIENCES AS DISTRICT JUDGE

Near-Fatal Meeting of Captain Cowan and the Nez Perce

Advent of the Automobile

Famous Water Cases

Looking Back on the District Judgeship

I have already mentioned that Mr. and Mrs. George Cowan of Boulder were friendly to me and we spent some time together when I was in their town on district court business. I had heard before about that family's incredible encounter with the Nez Perce Indians in 1877, but one day, when George Cowan rode with me in a one-horse buggy from Boulder to Elk Park to examine the premises involved in a water right suit, he told me the story in his own words and I would like to include it with my memoirs.

Cowan had been a young captain in the Union Army. After the war he came to Montana to practice law, settling first at Radersburg. At the mouth of Deep Creek canyon, on the road that afterward ran from Townsend to White Sulphur Springs, there dwelt a man named Carpenter, his wife and children, among the latter two lively girls. At the mouth of the canyon Nez Perce Indians under Chief Joseph camped on their expeditions to the Yellowstone for buffalo. Like other Indians at that time, the great chief's family begged from the settlers. The Carpenters supplied them as best they could. Although they did not know it at the time, they were "casting bread upon the waters."

Captain Cowan afterwards married the eldest Carpenter girl, a fine character. Being lively and adventurous young people, they planned a honeymoon trip to what is now our famous Yellowstone National Park, taking the other girl, a brother, and five others with them. All went well until they camped at a stream, afterwards known as Nez Perce creek, which flows into the Firehole River between the upper and lower geyser basins. The camp was not far from the Fountain geyser. The party had enjoyed a good night's sleep and were preparing breakfast, when some Indians came into camp. They were not truculent, rather pleasant.

Cowan had heard of the Nez Perce uprising in Idaho and that the Indians were coming to Montana, but he had no apprehensions about meeting them, certainly not in the National Park. That was supposed by the Indians, the whites said, to be at least an outpost of hell, with its sulphurous and other ill-smelling fumes, hot water and volcanic performances. The Indians, it was thought, feared the region and avoided it.

The Cowan party had met General Sherman and party the day before and had been informed about the Battle of the Big Hole and the advance of the Nez Perces. This naturally left a feeling of uneasiness in the minds of the Cowan party.

From here on I am telling Cowan's story as he told it to me. I am sensible that in some features it does not exactly agree with Mrs. Cowan's story as printed in Volume IV, Montana Historical Society Contributions, page 156. But this is the way he told it to me:

Some other Indians came on the scene and the Cowan party began to pack up. They were not hungry and the Indians were eating everything edible in sight. The Cowans wanted to kiss those Indians goodby. They didn't yet know they were Nez Perces. Mr. Cowan was packing some utensils and food in his camp kit in the wagon when 15 or 20 young men rode up, all heavily armed. They dismounted and went poking about the camp appropriating anything that struck their fancy. One came close to Cowan, reaching for something in the camp kit. Crossly, the Indian shoved Cowan from his path and Cowan knocked him to the ground.

Pandemonium broke loose, and it is a wonder all the whites were not killed instantly. Fortunately two older Indians rode up. One with a thunderous voice gave a command and the tumult ceased. Cowan went to these two and began to talk. One, Poker Joe, told

Cowan the man beside him of the mighty voice was Looking Glass. (This is pretty good proof that Looking Glass was not killed at the Battle of the Big Hole as some have asserted.)

Addressing himself to Looking Glass, Cowan began an impassioned appeal, pointing out that his was an inoffensive touring party knowing nothing of the war, and desirous of going in peace. Impassively, Looking Glass listened, said nothing. This chief was a large man, probably 5 feet 11 inches tall, if not full six feet, broad and muscular with a stolid Indian face. As Cowan proceeded with his appeal, another Indian rode up to Looking Glass, a little behind. He too was an impressive Indian, a little less than 5 feet 10 inches, very broad and muscular, dignified and stately. His face was intelligent and lordly. Looking Glass, indicating with thumb over his shoulder, said "Him Joseph."

Cowan then addressed his remarks to Joseph who said nothing, but he was taking in the scene. Seeing Mrs. Cowan and her sister, he smiled and directed that they be placed in custody of his own squaw, ordered that the others be taken in charge but kept in safety. Sullenly the Indians obeyed. Of course they took possession of horses, wagons and camp equipment belonging to the Cowan party and converted it to their own use. Mrs. Cowan and her sister were taken to Chief Joseph's campfire where Joseph's squaw looked after their wants. What white man in that day in the circumstances would have done as the great Chief Joseph did?

The story of the Battle of the Big Hole is one of the blackest pages in American history. I say this despite my admiration for General Gibbon, Captain Logan and Lieutenant Bradley. The battle was fought under a complete misapprehension of the policies and purposes of Chief Joseph. It was thought necessary to deal a crushing blow upon the Nez Perces under Chief Joseph, a fallacious notion. Some of the soldiers had in their minds the ancient idea of western man, frontiersmen, in settling the Indian problem: "Nits make lice." Peaceably, in what they supposed was the land of their friends, the Indians, including their wives and children, were sleeping in their camp on the North Fork of the Big Hole. Occasionally a baby would cry and its mother would soothe it. Then at daybreak the United States Army with some settlers of the Bitterroot shot down warriors, squaws and children in their teepees, killing many in their beds. A baby daughter of Chief Joseph was a victim. Despite this, the warriors running from their teepees to ascertain the cause of the uproar, fought their way back into their teepees, got their arms, and gave the Army and the settlers the worst licking in the history of Indian warfare next to the Custer disaster.

Poker Joe explained to Cowan without show of rancor, that in view of the Battle of the Big Hole, and especially in view of the fact that Montana men whom they supposed were friends fought with the Army, the hearts of the Nez Perces were bad, and Montana people were no longer safe. The next morning Poker Joe rode about the camp giving orders. The Cowan party was released with orders that they might go without molestation. They took the back trail and moved away from the Indians, but Cowan was uneasy. Noises began to reach him through the timber, slight at first but increasing. Soon he heard "Yip-yip-yip-yip-yip," and a group of young Indians including the one he had knocked down, rode near the Cowan party.

Two shots rang out and Captain Cowan slipped from his horse. Indians rushed toward him. Mrs. Cowan alighted and ran to him, observing blood spouting from his leg. Unable to stand, Cowan sank to the ground. Mrs. Cowan saw an Indian approaching with a large Navy revolver. The intention was clear; Cowan was to be killed. To protect her husband, Mrs. Cowan threw herself upon him, her arms around his neck. The Indian pulled back her head by the hair and shot Cowan in the forehead. The wound appeared ghastly, the blood flowed, and Cowan seemed to be dead.

In the meantime, Poker Joe was sent by the Chiefs to avoid trouble, they having apprehended that trouble was brewing. Poker Joe arrived just too late. Seeing the body of Cowan, he took Mrs. Cowan, her sister and brother back to the squaw camp. The other members of the Cowan party had escaped. That night while Mrs. Cowan was in the Chief Joseph tent, the great Indian leader sat by his campfire brooding, his fine face clear in the firelight. The squaw was tending her baby. Mrs. Cowan asked for it and her brother placed it in her lap. Chief Joseph smiled. While comforting the child, Mrs. Cowan broke into tears, and the squaw asked, "Why cry?" Young Cowan told the squaw his sister's husband had been killed that day. The squaw said, "She heartsick."

Without going into details, arrangements were made so that Mrs. Cowan, her sister and brother reached civilization and safety. Captain Cowan lay out in the sun, unconscious, until sometime in the afternoon. When consciousness returned he had a fierce thirst. A young pine tree grew nearby; reaching this, he pulled himself to a standing position. He had barely done so when he saw an Indian riding by, who pulled up his horse, took aim and shot Cowan through the thigh. Down he went, and out. It will be noted that he was not scalped on either occasion. The Nez Perces did not scalp as a rule, and none would have dared to take Cowan's fresh scalp into Chief Joseph's camp.

Sometime in the night, Cowan became conscious again. His thirst had not decreased. Painfully getting to his hands and knees, he reached water which restored him somewhat. The night was cold. When the sun finally warmed him, hunger set in. He crawled ten miles in four days and nights, finally reaching the camp where the Indians first approached. There he found some matches and coffee grounds but no food. Laboriously, he cooked up the coffee grounds and obtained something that tasted like coffee. Some time after that, while crawling on his hands and knees, he saw some men approaching on horseback. They were holding their guns in the prepare-to-shoot attitude. As he crawled toward them, he heard one say, "That's not an animal, it's a man." And another said, "It's a white man." Blood was all over his face, his clothes were disheveled and torn, and he could easily have been mistaken for an Indian.

The men were General Howard's scouts. Word was sent back for a surgeon, and General Howard, by means of a wagon sometimes pulled through or over a bad place by block and tackle, got him to a road. Eventually, after other adventures, one nearly fatal, he arrived at Bozeman, and fully recovered. Now this long story is hearsay with me, but Captain Cowan tried many cases before me, and was one of my best friends. I had heard this harrowing story as a boy. I am including it in my memoirs chiefly to paint a picture of what happened to two of my friends, Captain and Mrs. Cowan, in this Northwestern country when I was a boy nine years old.

ADVENT OF THE AUTOMOBILE

When I first became District Judge, our transport was much like the Cowans had used in 1877. But not long after the turn of the century, automobiles began coming into use and that made travelling easier. But one never knew in those days whether he could go from Virginia City to Dillon by auto without something happening. Always possible was a breakdown, a punctured tire, or what not. Judge Poindexter, who was of a thoughtful and cautious turn of mind, resolved to buy an auto. He knew mechanical principles generally, and after investigation concluded to buy a Cadillac, which he thought was the best of all mechanically. It cost him $1,800.00. The Buick was beginning to appeal to the public and was not considered expensive. But there was always something wrong with it. All that has since been overcome, and it is now a really good car.

The Model T Ford was the forerunner of the Cadillac and Buick and there were many of them. They had their troubles. My brother, Edmund, who had gone to Dillon to practice law, bought one. It was a funny contraption, as we look back to that time. Joe Poindexter brought me from Dillon to Virginia City in his Cadillac, and Edmund took me to and fro in his Ford. The Ford would stop. Edmund would get out and tinker with it, and after a while, for no apparent reason, the thing would go again.

We did not realize it until later, but a revolution was taking place. The horse and buggy were about to disappear. Horse ranches were to go. Our awful roads were to be made into modern highways. Travel was to become pleasant, joyous. Instead of freezing, enclosed cars with heaters in them now permitted the traveler to journey in comfort in severe weather. Ranchmen ceased to plod along country roads, humped up in the cold and wind, wasting time; instead they jump into their pick-up trucks and go speedily. Instead of the laborious freight wagons, drawn by oxen, horses, or mules, urged on by the bullwhacker or skinner with melodious and picturesque profanity, the swift truck whisks freight from place to place across the country.

FAMOUS WATER CASES

In my terms as District Judge, I tried many important water suits. I think I was the first judge in Montana to give comparatively small quantities of water to farmers as first rights, dividing the flood waters between them pro rata; awarding the use of waters by prescribing fixed periods of use in which the farmers must use the water alternately, and both methods have worked; encouraging the building of reservoirs, and in cases where the reservoirs were incomplete providing a time limit for their completion.

I personally measured water and ditch capacities during the trial of a water suit. After decree when there was a controversy, I visited the lands, ditches, and weirs and sought to adjust the difficulty. These procedures brought me some fame as a water right judge. But my successors have blamed me for my activities after decree, saying I created a precedent. But they are to blame. They have no business making water commissioners of themselves. I did not go that far.

As the political year 1912 came on, I thought of going on the Supreme Court, and discussed the subject with my friends. But as the campaign began to shape up, I changed my mind and decided to seek reelection as District Judge. This was assured. All the lawyers in the Fifth District agreed to re-nominate and re-elect Judge Poindexter and me without opposition—a Democrat and a Republican.

Meanwhile, Judge Winston of Anaconda, who had "swapped benches" with me frequently, asked me to try the Warm Spring Creek water suit; he said it would take me about two weeks. I accepted the invitation. A number of judges had been disqualified in the action. I found Judge Winston's estimate of the time involved was inaccurate.

There were a large number of lawyers working on the case and I remember many of them. Rodgers & Rodgers, W. B. Rodgers leading, did the principal work for the Anaconda Copper Mining Company; Robert L. Clinton and C. W. Sawyer represented the farmers, and various other interests employed T. P. Stewart. John James represented some defendants, Albert J. Galen the State Hospital, represented by J. M. Scanland, manager for the Mitchell interests.

As I remember, all the lawyers in Anaconda were in

the trial representing someone. The water involved included all that used by the Anaconda Company in Anaconda, the city of Anaconda, all the farmers along Warm Spring Creek, and the State Hospital at Warm Springs. Probably this suit involved more, so far as the value of water is reckoned, than any water suit ever tried in Montana. I took testimony for sixty days with a break for the purpose of attending the Spring convention of the Republican party at Livingston. That consumed about a week. After that we concluded taking testimony and adjourned for requested findings of fact.

THE HECTIC POLITICAL YEAR OF 1912

The district convention assembled and nominated me for District Judge. But when the office of Associate Justice came up in the deliberations, James A. Walsh of Helena in a eulogistic speech nominated me for that office. Many counties seconded the nomination. I took the platform and declined. I said we had talked it over at home, and I had announced to my friends that I would not accept the nomination. I had already been nominated for District Judge, I reminded them, and would be re-elected without opposition. They must name someone else. The convention would not take no for an answer and I was nominated by acclamation, after Beaverhead County and then Jefferson released me as a candidate for District Judge. In the circumstances I concluded to make the race, resigning my nomination for District Judge. Charles N. Pray, my future law partner, was nominated for Congress by acclamation, as was Henry C. Smith for the U.S. Senate.

In view of the terrible split in the Republican party with the emergence of the Bull Moose "Progressives" and the fact that the Democrats put up very strong candidates, it looked to me like a hopeless race. At that, if the Progressives had not nominated candidates for Congress and for Associate Justice (Thomas W. Everett and George W. Parr respectively), Pray and I would have been elected. But it was not to be. I went back to Virginia City to practice law in 1913, and the year following came our family move to Great Falls and some satisfying years practicing law.

LOOKING BACK ON THE DISTRICT JUDGESHIP

As I look back on a lifetime of working with the law and the judiciary, I must say that being a District Judge was a rare, human experience. The judge becomes an intimate figure in local life. His jurisdiction fills the gap between the Justice of the Peace and the Supreme Court. The most intimate affairs of the people of his district come before him. Accusations of crime, civil disputes, the estates of the incompetent and the dead, probate affairs, juvenile delinquency. Divorce presents the intimacies of human life in poignant aspects, especially when children by the marriage are concerned. Here the judge must employ his common sense, his humanity and of course his sympathy. Strangely enough, the sordid tendencies of mankind appear most frequently in contested probate matters, especially in will cases. I used to say that the meanest people with whom I had to deal were foreign heirs.

I had not anticipated difficulty in doing justice between man and man. I intended to do right. I thought that with study the judicial conscience would point to the truth, therefore the right way. But I overlooked the fact that in my country there were friendships between me and my constituents. Some were schoolmates, some were friends with whom I had ridden the range, others I had worked with for a day's pay. I might have anticipated that there would be litigation between some of these, and there was.

Generally the issues were clear enough and the right course was plain. The difficulty came when the cold neutrality of an impartial judge was required.

The danger here was to lean backward in an endeavor to be fair. On occasion I was reminded of the Missouri judge, who, on his way to court, met an intimate friend who asked in a tone of surprise, "Judge, you are not going to court today?" The judge answered in the affirmative. "Why," the friend persisted, "I thought the case today is between so and so as defendants." "It is." "How can you sit in that case? The defendant has been your bitter enemy for years." "Suh," said His Honor, "do you mean to impugn my integrity? I can give an enemy a fair trial. I can do more than that. I can give a friend a fair trial."

It may seem like a fancied recollection, but it is not. In such instances, I carried in my mind the maxim often heard among the cowboys: play fair. In deeper thought I would say to myself in moments of perplexity, "Here's where you must apply the Golden Rule." The results must have been fairly good. For example, after a most perplexing water suit, in which I had rendered a decree which I feared would bring upon me severe condemnation and offend some old friends, one of those in ranch clothes stopped his four-horse team in front of my residence on Cover Street, shouting "hello." When I came to the fence, he said, "What everybody says must be so." "How is that?" I inquired. He replied, "Well everybody says your decision in the Morgan Creek suit is as near right as it could be on the facts." I was gratified, as he as a comparative newcomer, among many users, must have hoped for an earlier right.

There were many opportunities to extend courtesies and favors when no one could be injured by extending them. By cultivating acquaintance, remembering first names, making friends with jurors and witnesses, a judge who renders good service is almost unbeatable. Each campaign rolled up large majorities for me. With this cogent expression of approbation, I liked my place as Fifth District Judge. Now I am sure it was the best position I ever held.

16

THE MOVE TO GREAT FALLS

Lucrative Law Practice in Virginia City
Nell's Need for Lower Altitude Living
My Esteemed Law Partner, Charles N. Pray
Law Partners in Other Towns
A New House and a Growing Practice
Educating Older Children and a New Baby Girl
Encounters With Charles M. Russell

The election was over with the inevitable result that there was presented to me an unusual opportunity. Sam V. Stewart had been elected Governor and Will A. Clark was to be Poindexter's co-adjutor. This left only Mont Duncan and George R. Allen as practicing attorneys in Virginia City. While on the campaign, I had looked over the cities of the state with an eye to a new location, having in mind Butte, Helena, Missoula and Great Falls. Not only was it dangerous to my wife's health (because of the altitude) to remain very long in Virginia City, but in that town the education facilities were not of the best.

Missoula would be good; its altitude was low and the schools excellent. The University was there. I did not know it, but I could have gone into partnership with a leading Missoula lawyer. I was offered a partnership in Helena and in Butte. From a business viewpoint, Butte was excellent. The three counties of my old district were tributary to it. No doubt large business would come to me from these counties, to say nothing of Butte itself. But the altitude of Butte was the same as Virginia City's and it seemed to Nell and me that Butte was not an attractive place for rearing children. Great Falls seemed to hold out promise, but I was almost unknown there.

We concluded to remain in Virginia City for a short time. I rented rooms for an office upstairs on Wallace Street midway of the block between Van Buren and Jackson Streets. The rooms were heated by a coal stove. Before I could get the place fitted up for service, clients were beating at the door. That year I look in $7,000.00 in cash and I had good business on the books. The practice that year was worth at least $10,000.00. I had been fortunate enough during the year, being in great need of a stenographer, to take on trial a red-headed girl named Pamela Brissette, whose parents lived in Ruby. She had learned the Pittman system, was smart, steady and faithful. She became one of the best stenographers I have ever known.

NELL'S NEED FOR LOWER ALTITUDE LIVING

We had our little white house on the hill in Virginia City from which we beheld the gorgeous sunsets, and were making money, but Nell's health was failing. I began to realize that while it would be difficult to leave the town and that attractive law business, we must get away. It would be pulling up the roots of our friendships and alliances, a tug on our heart strings. My mother was maintaining her residence in Virginia City and was fond of our children and they were fond of her.

Sometime in 1913, probably in the Spring, Nell and I went to Great Falls to consult Dr. Southmayd. Unfortunately, when we arrived, the doctor's daughter was seriously ill and we could not stay at the Southmayd home as their guests as had been the plan. The doctor got us rooms at the Rainbow Hotel. Nevertheless, we were at his house frequently during our stay in the city. Dr. Southmayd, upon consideration of Nell's case, said a prolonged rest was imperative, and it was determined that she should spend the summer with her mother and father at their ranch in Fergus County.

While in Great Falls, the doctor told me that Nell could not live at the high altitude of Virginia City, about 5,800 feet. Why not come to Great Falls, altitude 3,300, and establish a practice? It might be slow but he was sure that I would get business upon acquaintance—"when the people get to know you."

Shortly after that Nell, taking our youngest, Llewellyn (Pete), went to Fergus County, arriving in Lewistown on September 12, 1913, the boy's sixth birthday.

Nell's brother, Woodson, met them in a buckboard at the railroad and drove them to the ranch. The long vacation on the ranch was beneficial, but it would have been foolish to remain living in Virginia City. My recollection is that Nell and I went to Great Falls again in 1913, at which time we bought a lot at 1400 Third Avenue North from Dr. and Mrs. J. H. Irwin, who later became our close friends.

MY ESTEEMED LAW PARTNER, CHARLES N. PRAY

I had known Charles N. Pray since the campaign of 1906, if not before. As we have seen, he was a candidate for re-election to Congress in 1912, and of course we met in that campaign. Sometime in 1913, we passed a few letters. I met him at the Park Hotel in December 1913, as I remember, to discuss joining for practice in Great Falls. We took a long walk in Gibson Park talking it over. I had now practiced practically a year since leaving the Fifth Judicial District bench. He had been out of practice seven years, the six years he had spent in Congress and a year following due to his wife's distressing health. We agreed to join forces, using our names, Charles N. Pray and Lew L. Callaway. I went back to Virginia City to break up my office.

LAW PARTNERS IN OTHER TOWNS

Now I made an interesting connection. A young lawyer, Howard P. Beckett, smart but very green, had come to Sheridan with his young wife, Helen. Both were natives of Peabody, Massachusetts, a suburb of Boston. Both were descendants of those who came to America originally on the Mayflower. Both talked a Bostonese of the educated type. Harvard was pronounced Haavaad by both. The young couple, married not altogether with their parents' blessing, had gone to Canada seeking a location but had ended up in Sheridan, Montana. It was certainly a much safer town to live in than Peabody, pronounced "Pea Buddy," but Sheridan was a western town and in the view of far Easterners, dangerous. Howard and Helen slept their first night in Sheridan with a butcher knife under Howard's pillow.

Howard Beckett was not the man I would have chosen in ordinary circumstances, but I just had to have someone in charge of my Madison County office. So I made him a proposition: he and his wife would live in our house, I would leave him some of my office furniture and some law books, and we made some arrangement about fees—I don't remember what it was. The firm name would be Callaway & Beckett. I then shipped the bulk of my law books to Great Falls, and Charles Pray and I opened offices in the Tod Building (afterwards the Stanton Bank Building) in January 1914.

I had entered into a partnership with my brother Edmund at Dillon under the name of Lew L. & E. J. Callaway. This arrangement was that I would do the trial work for the firm as Edmund asked me to do it, and I would share in the proceeds from the trials in which I took part; all the other Beaverhead fees would go to him.

A NEW HOUSE AND A GROWING PRACTICE

I owned stock in the Elling State Bank and in its subsidiary, the Southern Montana Bank at Ennis, and was a director in both. Borrowing $6,000.00 from Horace Elling with my Elling State Bank stock as security, I commenced the building of a house on the lot I had bought in Great Falls. We moved into our house at 1400 Third Avenue North on August 31, 1914, my wife's birthday.

Remaining in Great Falls a few days in January 1914, I soon had to go back to Virginia City and Dillon for trial work. After the trials I would return to Great Falls. In the years 1914, 1915 and perhaps 1916, I used up two 3,000 mile books on the railroads each year. I tried cases in Madison and Beaverhead Counties every year, almost uniformly successful. The cases in Jefferson and Silver Bow Counties were water suits.

Gradually, I worked into trials in Cascade, Choteau, Teton, Glacier, Fergus and other counties. It sounds like boasting to tell the fact that I seldom lost a case. Charlie Pray, better adapted to trial work than I was, seldom tried a case; he became an office man. He was not inclined to mix, yet he was a marvelous mixer. Everyone seemed to like him. He seldom went to Havre or Fort Benton that he did not return with new business.

The political leaders tried to get my partner to run for Congress in 1914, but I talked him out of it. I saw certain defeat ahead. The fetish of Woodrow Wilson was strong that year, and Charlie, as a Republican, could not have won. Before I could prevent it, the Republicans got him into the race for the Senate in 1916. He won the nomination but he was defeated in the election by Henry Myers by 7,000 votes. It was very difficult for Charlie to get back into practice. Sometimes he would pound the desk and say he could never do it. He had been a grand Congressman, engrossed with his work, patriotic to a remarkable degree. If he had a federal case to look up, something would remind him of his service in Congress, and in his own mind he would be fighting the old battle over again. "I can't make it, I tell you; I can't make it."

But Charlie Pray made it. There never was a better office associate. He never complained of my absences, rather encouraged them, even if he had no share in the fees, and exulted over my victories. He was the very embodiment of unselfishness. After a while on my insistence, we adopted a firm name of Pray & Callaway, afterward Pray, Callaway & Toole.

Along in the Spring of 1914, I said to Pam Brisette that I would take her to Great Falls and increase her salary if she would come; she said she would if I wanted her. And so she did. Working for Mr. Pray and me for more than six years, she married which led her to quit our employ. She was a devout Catholic but unusually close mouthed. I dictated my Masonic correspondence to her, and while there was nothing secret about it, I am satisfied that no gentleman of the clergy could have pried any of it from her by any means. She was amiable, modest, a high minded and highly moral woman. Work increased in the office so we took on added clerical help at times.

One day a young man came in saying, "My name is Warren Toole. I want a job." He did not say, "I am the son of Governor Toole, the nephew of E. W. Toole." I asked him if he was the son of Governor Toole, and he said yes. We employed and retained him until he went to war and took him back when he returned. He was a sound thinker, industrious and a good briefer.

EDUCATING OLDER CHILDREN & A NEW BABY GIRL

I mentioned Charlie Pray's generosity. One of his old acquaintances, an elderly lady, brought him an estate that should have paid him $1,000.00, probably more. He worked away at the estate, but never got anything from her. There came a time when I needed money very badly. Building the house and afterwards having Miriam at Wheaton College and Jimmy at Staunton Military Academy in Virginia, had seriously depleted my resources. Our youngest child, Mary Elizabeth, arrived in the Spring of 1917 and a new baby is always a source of expense. God knows we loved her.

I was complaining about the collections and the need for money when one morning Charlie gave me a check for $400.00. I asked him where he got it, and he said it was part of the estate fee. I congratulated him on collecting the fee, afterwards ascertaining that he had not collected a cent of it. He drew that money out of his personal funds.

ENCOUNTERS WITH CHARLES M. RUSSELL

Life in Great Falls was becoming increasingly enjoyable. We joined the Fortnightly Dancing Club. We were also members of a smaller dancing club organized in the neighborhood. The Irwins, Charles M. Russells, George Sutherlands and a number of others belonged to it. Some of these, with others, got up a dinner-dance club. It was the custom of this club to have supper during the evening. One night we went to this club as guests of the Dows. The Russells were there and Charlie began telling stories. He had a marvelous faculty as a yarn spinner, and that night he was at his best. Perhaps we were at the table two or three hours, laughing a good deal of the time.

The first time I saw Charles Russell was in 1908 when the Elks were having their first state convention in Great Falls. We were, a large number of us, dancing on Central Avenue, soon drifting into the Silver Dollar Saloon, one of Russell's favorite places. There I saw behind the bar his famous painting showing Indians entertaining a cowboy.

I formally met Russell and his wife, Mame, shortly after Mr. Pray and I opened our office. Charlie Pray said he had been drawing up a contract whereby the Russells were renting his pictures to a concern which was to make lithographs of them. He had an appointment at the Russell home, and would I like to go along? I would, so we went to the Russell residence on Fourth Avenue North. We were invited in by Mrs. Russell, very graciously. I was introduced; Mrs. Russell bade me welcome. When introduced as Judge Callaway to Charles Russell, he said "umph" and shut up like a clam. Mrs. Russell and Mr. Pray discussed the contract which she pronounced satisfactory.

This done, Mr. Pray saw a canvas on an easel, a painting just finished. It showed a cowboy who had his lariat over the head and one front leg of a large yearling; the yearling was on one side of the ravine, the cowboy on the other, with a cow running down the ravine encountering the rope, one end of which was around the yearling and the other tied to the saddlehorn. The cowboy was leaning out of the saddle with his spur in the cantle of the saddle in an effort to keep his saddle from turning. Mr. Pray inquired about what was happening in the picture. Since Mr. Russell said nothing, I explained the situation. "You've been there, have you?" Russell said, and when I told him I had ridden the range working with cattle for years, he became loquacious and we were friends thereafter. Later I went to his studio frequently, usually on Sunday mornings when he was varnishing his paintings. He would squat on his heels while doing the work, telling stories as he did so.

After a painting was finished, he would talk of it impersonally. For example, he had presented to the Elks Lodge in Great Falls, after his initiation, a large painting called "The Exalted Ruler." It showed a magnificent antlered elk on a hill with the herd about him. In the distance were lofty mountains with the brilliant colors one sees sometimes at sunrise or sunset. I asked whether it was sunrise or sunset; I said I wasn't sure. Being at the Lodge with Charlie, I asked him to accompany me to the picture and when we were before it, asked him the question, "Is it sunrise or sunset?" He said, "Damned if I know. Sunrise I guess."

He put his trademark, a buffalo skull, on his paintings. But when I saw the large painting in the House of Representatives in the capital in Helena, instead of the buffalo skull he had painted the skull of a mountain sheep. The picture depicts the Lewis and Clark party trading for horses with the Indians in Ross' Hole. I asked Russell why he had painted the sheep's skull instead of the buffalo's, and he said, "Because there were no buffalo in that part of the country." Historically correct. Russell was meticulous about history. On inspection of any of his paintings you will find saddle, bridle, gun or any object depicted faithfully in accord with the period.

Charles M. Russell's "Rawhide Rawlins," "Trails Plowed Under" and other books are mainly stories collected from the lore of the time, regardless of authorship. One day I met him on Central Avenue in Great Falls after one of his books came out, and said, "Say, you swiped one of my stories." "Which one?" "That one where the Indians chased that feller up the box canyon." "Huh," he said, "I heard that one before I ever met you." One fall, Russell, Frank Linderman, John E. Lewis and Irwin S. Cobb went camping near Chief Mountain. Afterwards I read some of Russell's stories told by Cobb with literary embellishment in a magazine.

Charlie Russell had not had much schooling, but he was a long way from being as ignorant in the use of English as he pretended. He was much better informed about many subjects than most men are. It was the fact that he preserved so much Montana history with such discrimination in his paintings that led the University of Montana to honor him with an LL.D. In addition to his skill as an illustrator (that's what he said he was) and an artist in oils and watercolors, he was a natural sculptor of unusual ability. It was his habit to carry in his coat pocket some modeling clay. He often worked with this as he talked. It was amazing to see the results of what appeared mere careless play on the part of this remarkable man and artist whom I had the privilege of coming to know during our residence in Great Falls.

A BUSY LIFE IN GREAT FALLS

I became a member of the Commercial Club in Great Falls and was elected a director and president. I also joined a highbrow club of which Harry B. Mitchell, later U. S. Civil Service Commissioner, I. Parker Veasy, Jr., Edgar Mackay and others of that type were members. The dinners were intellectual as well as gustatory feasts.

I was prominent in Great Falls Masonic circles from the time I was speaker at the laying of the cornerstone of the temple in June 1914, until I left the city. While there I was elected Grand High Priest of the Grand Royal Arch Chapter of the state, and Grand Commandery of the Grand Conclave of Knights Templar, having received this last election on Melita Island in Flathead Lake. The Inspector General, Edward C. Day of Helena, established Scottish Rite bodies in Great Falls in 1919. I was a member of the first class, 35 in number, and was elected its president.

I did not seek political office during my residence in Great Falls until 1922. But I was elected president of the Montana Bar Association at the annual meeting held in Missoula in 1916, and in 1917 was appointed a member of the State Board of Law Examiners by the Supreme Court, later becoming its chairman. For five years I was president of the Cascade County Bar Association.

Ahead in my destiny loomed once more the Montana Supreme Court.

17

CHIEF JUSTICE OF THE MONTANA SUPREME COURT

Campaigning for the High Court

Lawyer in the Morning, Chief Justice in the Afternoon

A Near-Fatal Bout With Peritonitis

On Becoming Chief Justice

A Quiz for the Chief Justice

During political campaigns I made speeches in Cascade County. In 1920 I also spoke in Teton, Pondera, and Choteau Counties. But I never was an extra good campaign speaker. I doubt if I was entitled to be called good. I tried to talk sense and avoid "hooey," and to please a political crowd the impression was that one had to indulge in more or less—more I think—"hooey," or spout sophomoric oratory.

For many years I had dreams of becoming U. S. Senator or Governor or Chief Justice. I am thankful now that I never was Senator or Governor. The political conditions in Montana and in most of the other states after 1910 were never promising to a believer in the U.S. Constitution. The fact is that the United States has been rushing into socialism ever since 1899. In Montana since 1894, what with the copper war, socialism, the Bull Moose idiocy, the "new freedom," and worst of all the "New Deal." A believer in sensible and practical government has been in hot water pretty constantly.

In 1922, although apprehensive over Judge Theodore Brantly's health, we induced him to file for re-nomination for Chief Justice and, in ordinary circumstances, he would have been re-elected. But in July 1922, it became apparent that he would be unable to make the campaign or to discharge the duties of Chief Justice if he were elected.

His wife, who was my cousin, Lois, telephoned me in July that the Judge could not go on and urged me to file for the nomination. I did not have much time because in those days we had to procure nominating petitions from all over the state. But after I announced that I would be a candidate, my friends in Great Falls got up a club and we put on a vigorous campaign. No one had filed against Judge Brantly except an unqualified man in Havre. Judge Brantly aided my campaign in every way he could and all was progressing nicely when Governor Dixon, for whom I had made speeches in 1920, got on the telephone and, at the state's expense, induced his appointee as Associate Justice, George Farr, to file for Chief Justice. The campaign really got warm.

A few days later I was in Helena and met Governor Dixon (whom I had always called Joe) in the Capitol. We shook hands. He asked, "What are you doing here?" and I replied, "Running for office." "Who's running against you?" was the Governor's next question, and I said, "George Farr, but I am going to be nominated." The vote came on August 29 and I had a plurality of over 12,500.

LAWYER IN THE MORNING, CHIEF JUSTICE IN THE AFTERNOON

Judge Brantly died on September 16, 1922, and I got the news at Edmund's house in Dillon. I went to Helena for the funeral and then returned to Great Falls. On September 28 I argued a case before the Supreme Court, beginning my argument at 10:00. Before the argument was finished, the Governor's private secretary, Will Aiken, came to me in the courtroom, saying the Governor wanted to see me. As soon as the argument was finished, I met Governor Dixon in his private secretary's office.

"What do you think I should do? Should I appoint you Chief Justice?" the Governor asked. I said, "I think you should appoint me. I am the nominee of the Republican Party." "Well," he said, "I guess I'd better appoint you." Turning to Mr. Aiken, the Governor said, "Make out Judge Callaway's commission as Chief Justice." I qualified immediately. Thus I had what I think is a unique record, for I have never heard of a similar case: I argued a case before the Supreme

Court in the morning and took my seat on the bench as Chief Justice at 2:00 on the same day.

Shortly after that I started upon my regular campaign with Dan Boyle, candidate for Railroad Commissioner. I do not remember much about the campaign for reasons that will appear. My opponent was Joseph Jackson, a District Judge from Butte, a good lawyer and a decent man.

I remember spending a night in Bainville in eastern Montana. The town was crowded for some reason and we could not get a bed, so we spent the night, or that part of it we did not pass, walking around town, sitting in hard chairs in the hotel office. From Bainville we took the Great Northern train to Great Falls, intending to go to Helena. My wife came to the train in Great Falls and we talked a few minutes. I was to see her again soon, unexpectedly. We went on to Helena.

A NEAR-FATAL BOUT WITH PERITONITIS

I was tired, retiring early in my room at the Placer Hotel. About 1:00 in the morning I awoke with a terrific pain in the sternum. It was as if an Indian had crawled over the transom and buried his tomahawk into me. I suffered a severe chill. For a time it was impossible to get out of bed, and when I did, I could not stand up, could not reach the telephone on the wall. By intense effort I reached the push button that summoned the bellboy.

I told him my trouble and said I must have a doctor. After futile tries, he was unable to reach doctors I had consulted in other days. Finally, he reached Dr. Lanstrum, who was at a party. The doctor came in his party clothes. He gave me a hypodermic, telling me to stay in bed until he came again, which he did about 9:30 in the morning. He said he had arranged to take me to St. Peter's Hospital. I protested, telling him I was right in the middle of my campaign. That made no difference, he said, I must go to the hospital at once.

So, taking a cab, the doctor and I went. The nurses undressed me, put on a night gown that buttoned up the back, and stowed me in bed.

Dr. Lanstrum came with his associate, Dr. Brooke.

I knew Dr. Brooke's reputation; he was supposed to be a cutter. He said I had appendicitis and an immediate operation was indicated. I brought up the campaign, insisting that sickness now might be fatal to my hopes. Dr. Brooke said I might end up a real fatality if I did not have the operation at once. But after further talks, the doctors thought they could break up the attack with ice packs. I lay all that day pretty nearly frozen but to no avail. Dr. Brooke said he would have to operate. I said I would not permit it until Dr. Southmayd approved. This decision saved my life.

Dr. Southmayd got word late in the afternoon and as soon as he and my wife got ready—a very short time—they left Great Falls in a taxi, drove all night, a distance of 100 miles in heavy rain, through gumbo and dirt roads, reaching St. Peter's at 4:00 in the morning. Dr. Southmayd asked if a blood count had been taken; no, it had not. He arranged for it, waking up an employee of the State Board of Health.

The blood count left no doubt of the need for a speedy operation. I rather enjoyed taking the ether, and came out of it without distress. The appendix had burst and Dr. Southmayd said I had the wildest peritonitis he ever saw. The operation over, Dr. Brooke started to sew up the incision but Dr. Southmayd insisted that he put in a number of drainage tubes. Dr. Brooke said it was no use. One of my nurses later told me, "When Dr. Brooke started to sew you up, I thought Dr. Southmayd was going to jump out the window."

Dr. Brooke pronounced my case hopeless and told my wife so. She disagreed and they had a vigorous row over it. Dr. Southmayd said I had about one chance in a hundred. On the train the next morning he told a friend I had about one chance in a thousand. I soon fell into a prolonged delirium, during which I had terrific experiences. Dr. Southmayd came back in a day or two to see how I was getting along. He wouldn't take a cent for all his services or expenses. Dr. Landstrum had employed Miss Pache, whom he thought was the best nurse in town, and another good woman. Eventually, the peritonitis cleared up. I had indeed been a very sick man, had been at the point of death for days.

The attack had hit me about October 19 or 20. I was elected in November while still in a dangerous condition. In the first week of December I was able to go to Great Falls, returning to Helena in the closing days of the month. My memory was gone for a time. But gradually it returned, in most particulars. But the memories of the 1922 campaign itself are gone for all time.

ON BECOMING CHIEF JUSTICE

On the first Monday of January, 1923, I took my seat as Chief Justice and carried on my work. Strange how things work out. All the doctors who had anything to do with my case, including the man who took the blood count, and Dr. Treacy, an associate of Drs. Landstrum and Brooke, are all dead. Landstrum died in 1928. I attended the funeral of Dr. Southmayd, my best friend, years ago. No one there, including his wife and children, suffered more than I did.

The work of the Supreme Court was difficult but I had three very good judges, William L. Holloway, Albert J. Galen, and Albert P. Stark. Charles H. Cooper, the other Associate Justice, was an accident, not a good lawyer, but a good companion. He was the father of the well known actor, Gary Cooper. This is not the place to enter into a discussion of the technique of the work, nor the quality of the opinions. We did right or as near right as it was possible for us to do. We were not "influenced" by any human being so far as I know. Honorable John A. Matthews succeeded Judge Cooper in 1925.

As Chief Justice I attended the American Law Institute in Washington, D.C. in 1923, 1924, and 1925, meeting many of the great judges and lawyers of the country.

This is the end of Judge Callaway's memoirs. Chapter 18, written by L. L. Callaway, Jr., will describe the later years of the Judge's life.

A QUIZ FOR THE CHIEF JUSTICE

Editor's Note: Following are excerpts from a hearing by the Economy Committee of the House of Representatives. They include the Judge's answers to a series of questions put to him on January 24, 1933, about the financial status and the history of the Montana Supreme Court. His answers reveal much about Judge Callaway: his sense of fiscal and legal responsibility, his dedication to public service, and his sense of humor. The questions were put to him by S. H. Knowles, L. A. Nutting, V. F. Blankenbaker, and Peter Hilger, members of the Committee.

Q. I would like you to give an account of the salaries in your department.

A. Since when?

Q. We want the whole history, and the costs for the last fifteen years.

A. There has been no raise in judicial salaries in the Supreme Court since 1905. Montana is one of eight states that did not raise the judicial salaries either during or after the war. The Supreme Court of Montana has less help than any state west of the Mississippi River (unless it be Utah), and has had less help for the last ten years as far as I know, with the exception of Arkansas, according to information furnished me. In all of the states west of the Mississippi, except Montana and Utah, each Judge has either one stenographer or a law clerk, who is also a stenographer. Washington is an exception to that; Washington has six law clerks for seven Judges, Idaho has five for five men, and Colorado has seven for seven men. Utah pays its Judges $5,000.00 per year and it has three law clerks, who are stenographers and deputy clerks for five men. Utah has one case submitted three years ago not decided, and a good many cases argued two years ago and not decided, and I do not know how many others argued and not decided. Montana, by having efficient help and working overtime, has been practically up-to-date for the last ten years, and all of the cases that have been argued and submitted to the Supreme Court have been decided with the exception of one which is in the hands of a district judge, which was argued in October, and cases argued in January. There was a period in our history when this Court was behind because of insufficient help and an insufficient number of Judges, and the Legislature had to create commissions; but there has been no commission since July, 1923, as we have been able to keep up. We ran behind this last year on account of special proceedings that were initiated in this Court. Some questions presented to us have never been before any Court for decision, and are just as difficult as those which are brought before the Supreme Court of the United States.

We have a Marshal and always have had for the last thirty years or longer. His salary was raised in 1919 from $125.00 per month to $150.00. We had a fine man, as an individual, here at that time, Marshal Race, but he was just an ordinary Court Marshal who opened the Court and adjourned it, and kept order; in his latter years most of his time was spent lying on the lounge in the corridor; we did not have the heart to turn him out. He died in 1924 and we concluded that we would see if we could get something for the money, so we determined we would appoint as Marshal someone qualified to become a law clerk; so we selected a recent graduate of the University of Montana, and stipulated he should help as a law clerk. After a while he went up to Havre, and is county attorney there now. We took on another man because he was a disabled veteran, but he did not render the service expected, and he quit about the middle of May, I believe; so we decided to get along without a Marshal until after the summer vacation. During two bienniums we have saved $600.00 by getting along without a Marshal for a short time, although he is allowed by statute.

Q. You did not take all the expenses allowed by statute?

A. No. And except once, years ago, we have never used any of our traveling expenses. Usually $100.00 a year has been allowed.

Q. You have never used any of it?

A. No, except as stated. We have made no request for it in this budget, hoping there will not be any need for it. I will explain that situation so you will see it more clearly. Once in a while it is necessary for the Supreme Court to issue a writ to a public officer. We had one this year, but the officer was here in the Capitol and there was no expense. In this connection the Marshal is entitled to the same compensation for the service of papers, if I recall correctly, as a sheriff is.

Q. You do not really need this money?

A. Not unless a proposition of that kind arises. We hope it will not. The Marshal has not been paid any fees by the State for serving papers during the last five or six years, and I do not recall a time in the last ten years. In a case this year the parties insisted on sending the Marshal to Butte to serve the papers, and the mileage was about $19.00, and that is all the Marshal received outside of his salary, to my recollection.

Judge Matthews: I think he served some papers in the Lasby case, for which he was paid $7.00 by the parties.

Chief Justice Callaway: I overlooked that.

Q. The salary of the Marshal is fixed by law?

A. Yes.

Q. Is it just a ruling that he be a law clerk?

A. Yes. Then we have a court attendant. There has been a court attendant ever since I first came to the Court in 1903, and there was one before that. He received $100.00 per month by appropriation. It is not an office created by law. In 1913, I think it was, the Legislature provided that the court attendant might act as clerk in the absence of the clerk. And the Legislature gave him $40.00 in addition; so that gave him $140.00 per month. At that time the clerk was John T. Athey, who was growing elderly, and he was sick occasionally. Yes, it was 1913 that the law was enacted. It reads: "Whenever the Clerk of the Supreme Court is incapacitated or absent, the attendant of the Supeme Court is hereby authorized to perform all of the functions and duties of said clerk."

Q. What section is that?

A. That is section 377. Ward Crosby, the present clerk, had a leg shot off in the war, and the other leg is none too good. He has a wooden leg, and every little while he has to go away and have an expert firm fit a new leg. The attendant acts as clerk in his absence. The attendant is Oliver T. Crane.

Q. Is the clerk properly an employee of the Supreme Court?

A. He belongs to this department, but he is an elective officer.

Q. Does the salary go on while he is away?

A. Yes, of course.

Q. Does the Clerk of the Supreme Court have a stenographer?

A. No. We permit Mr. Crane to help out in the clerk's office.

Q. What other help is there?

A. We have two stenographers; that is all the help we have. Mr. Schneider came with the Court in 1896, and I do not think he can be duplicated in the United States. He is of great assistance in reporting the decisions, and up to now has taken all the testimony necessary in the Court. This morning we had Mr. Marvin take down proceedings in Court. Mr. Schneider engrosses all the opinions, and is the official stenographer of the Court. His compensation rested upon appropriations for a good many years. Years ago he was, as I remember, given $2,400.00, then $2,600.00, once $2,800.00, and he got some small amounts from furnishing copies, but he is a very busy man and works longer than any other man in the Capitol. In order to give him adequate compensation, we used to pay him out of our own salaries. We paid him $200.00 per year apiece. We talked the matter over with the members of the Legislature, and they thought we should not pay for our help ourselves and that there should be an increase in his salary, if we did not ask too much. Thereupon the Legislature, in 1929, fixed his salary at $4,000.00. In the meantime court reporters had been getting $3,000.00 per year and transcript work. Mr. Marvin, a court reporter, tells me he made about $4,500.00 per year—so Schneider does not get so much. That is, the court reporters made that much when business was good.

We cannot get along here with ordinary help; the ordinary stenographer cannot function here. Some stenographers think it is so, but it is not. We have to have expert help, as it is technical work. Our stenographers have to be people in whom we have the highest confidence; they must be above suspicion. Court secrets must not get away; they have got to be personally satisfactory to the people for whom they work, and they have much work to do. The ordinary person cannot do it. We were lucky enough to get Judge Law's stenographer temporarily for $150.00. He served Judge Stark and Judge Law for fifteen years, and when Judge Law went out of the public service, we got him. We cannot expect to keep that kind of man for $150.00 per month. I believe now that I have told you about all of our employees.

Now the Justices of this Court are not like, in duties, any other Justices west of the Mississippi River. We discharge the ordinary functions of Justices of the Supreme Court, but in addition to that we report the decisions. That is an additional burden the Legislature could not compel us to discharge, but which the

Court is willing to discharge. Prior to 1899, this Court did what all others Courts do. Well, the different reporters which the Court had employed, while they were excellent men, did not satisfy everybody, and they were expensive considering the work done. In 1899 the Court had three unusual men: Judge Brantly, probably the greatest brain serving on the bench in the State at any time; Judge Hunt, and Judge Pigott. They were paid $4,000.00 per year each. The Legislature wanted to increase the salaries of Justices, but could not do so under the Constitution; and they hit on the device of making the Judges the reporters, thus doing away with the Court Reporter system which nobody liked. And so they passed an act paying the Justices $1.500.00 per year for reporting the decisions, and thus in effect raised their salaries. This made their salaries $5,500.00. Since that time every Justice has been elected with that salary standing on the books.

Q. The salary was four thousand dollars?

A. Yes. In 1905 District Judges' salaries were raised to $4,000.00 and Justices' salaries to $6,000.00 and thus the two salaries ran. All Justices have been elected receiving both these salaries.

Q. Are both protected by the Constitution?

A. Yes, certainly.

Q. It could not be changed by an act?

A. No, not during the term of these present officers. At that, we receive less than do the Justices of most of the Supreme Courts in the United States. Some get more and some get less. I have a classmate on the Supreme Court of Colorado and from him have been informed how much they are getting there. They each get $5,000.00 a year, but they do not do anything but act as Justices. The Supreme Court of Colorado is a year and a half behind in its work. We have had no trouble in this Court about back work.

Q. What I want to know is the salary here.

A. We get $6,000.00 and $1,500.00, or $7,500.00, set by law. Set by two different sections, and both are under the Constitution.

Q. The $1,500.00 salary was set in 1899, but the legal salary was raised?

A. The last raise was in 1905. The Constitution provides that the salary of a Justice shall neither be raised or diminished during his term of office.

I, Lew L. Callaway, Chief Justice of the Supreme Court of Montana, hereby certify, in my official capacity, that the foregoing transcript of a statement made by me before the Honorable Economy Committee of the House of Representatives on January 24, 1933, is, in so far as my testimony was taken down by the stenographer, and as corrected by me, in all respects true and correct.

18

THE LATER YEARS

BY L. L. CALLAWAY, JR.

1934: Heartbreak Year

A Healing Trip

Triumph Over Illness

Meaningful Work and the Later Years

Nell Callaway: Beloved Survivor

Nineteen thirty-four was the most heartbreaking year for the Callaway family.

In August our beloved Frances Lathrop Callaway was killed in an automobile accident. Both the Judge and Nell were devastated. This was the first loss in the family and one of the most tragic. She left a one-year old son, sturdy and bright. Fan, the second daughter of the Judge and Nell, was a lovely, talented and vivacious woman. When she entered a room, her lively presence was felt immediately. She was a strong and vibrant personality. Her education had included a year at Mills College, Oakland, California and the University of Montana, at Missoula. (Her son, Samuel Dupuy Goza, III, grew to be a nice looking 6′2″ man with a delightful sense of humor and smart enough to become an M.D. He married a fine woman, Janice Sherwood and was the father of three sons and a daughter.)

Then came the election in November, which went overwhelmingly for the Democrats throughout the nation. It was the well-known "Roosevelt Landslide." Chief Justice Callaway ran for re-election on the Republican ticket and was defeated. Normally he would have been the Chief Justice for life, but this was the fifth year of the Great Depression.

January, 1935 found Lew Callaway, age 67, with no job, no income, and of course, no pension. Besides Nell his wife, and Mary Elizabeth his daughter, the family also included our oldest sister Miriam and her two sons (Harper L. Jones and L. L. Jones) who had come to live in the house on Lawrence in 1926, when one was two years old and the other a baby. (The boys were supported by my father until they went to college and were, of course, happy additions to the family.)

My father was faced with the necessity of starting his law practice again, in the wake of the worst depression the nation had ever endured. At 67 it was a prospect to daunt the most fearless. His feelings were not made any brighter, eventually, by the dismal record of his successor as Chief Justice, who wrote only two opinions in his six years in office.

The Judge opened his law office in the Union Bank Building. Gradually, clients came to his door. His many friends did everything they could to help. Mary Elizabeth immediately got a job at the Capitol and, later, with Western Life Insurance Company, and Miriam also worked.

A HEALING TRIP

Luckily, I was hired by *Time* magazine in May, 1937. This was a step upward for me in magazine publishing, where I had started with Condé Nast in 1932. After graduation from Dartmouth and earning an MBA at Harvard Business School, I was assigned to *Time*'s Chicago office. This new job meant that for the first time in my life I had some extra money. At once I invited the Judge and my mother to come to Chicago in June. My proposal was that since I had to go east to my first *Time* sales meeting, my wife and I would take them with us and they would not have to spend a dime after they reached Chicago. We would drive east in my new Chevrolet and stop first at the University of Michigan, in Ann Arbor, where my father had gone to law school. We would then go by ship to Buffalo; drive across New York for an overnight stay at Saratoga Springs; and then proceed to Hanover, New Hampshire, to visit Dartmouth, my college, which neither of my parents had ever seen.

It was hard trying to convince my father to agree to the trip because he was broke and had not yet recovered from the terrible events of 1934. In any event, my parents finally arrived at Union Station, and my wife Helene and I met them. The Judge was worn to a frazzle. He was not like his old self and did not smile or laugh for almost a week.

Ann Arbor was a big disappointment to my father because he did not recognize a single building that had been there when he was in law school. They had all disappeared. They had been removed to make way for the splendid new buildings of today's University of Michigan.

Our trip across the lake to Buffalo was just wonderful. Finally, when we were settled in one of those great old Victorian suites at one of the grand old hotels in Saratoga (I think it was the "United States Hotel"), my father started to relax. He finally laughed at someone's joke and from that time on, he was his old self again. He was essentially a man of great good humor, and it was a wonderful relief to all of us to see him throw off the pall which had seemed to hang over him.

To see the gleaming halls of Dartmouth for the first time was a big thrill for my mother and father. One of the oldest of the New England colleges, it is almost a "picture book" college. All of its buildings, with a few exceptions, are Georgian architecture, and the appearance is very beautiful. We stayed at the Hanover Inn with nice rooms and good food. We took several tours of the campus, the Baker Library, Massachusetts Row, where I roomed for three years, and many other places dear to me. Our trip to Dartmouth was a huge success.

From there we drove to Westport, Connecticut, where my wife's sister, Mrs. John Chapman, lived in a beautiful old 1720 house. This is where my little family lived while I went off to my first *Time* sales meeting at Virginia Beach.

After my return to Westport, we had an easy and pleasant trip back to Chicago, where my parents took the famous—at the time—"North Coast Limited" (Northern Pacific) back to Helena. This entire expedition did my psyche a lot of good and seemed to bring a real recuperation to both of my parents. I have always been so happy about that great trip we all took together.

TRIUMPH OVER ILLNESS

In 1939, my father had a severe stroke, which among other things, affected his speech. He stayed home with nurses. It was a wearing and expensive time. We all wondered how the family made it through all the problems. His head nurse Mrs. Mundt said, "The Judge had a perfect mental attitude for one afflicted as he was at the time." There was no loss of his mental powers following the stroke. He knew he was going to recover from the stroke. And he did.

My sister Mary Elizabeth was scheduled to be married to Dr. Gordon L. Doering on September 14, 1939. About five days after his stroke, my father called Mary, my oldest sister Mimi and my mother to his room. Although he had great difficulty in speaking, he insisted that the wedding go ahead as planned. From this fortunate union have arrived five wonderful children: Charles, Jean Randolph, Bruce Callaway, Mary Ellen, and Thomas Doering.

After we entered the war against Germany and Japan and Italy, my sister Mimi wrote me saying, "There are only old men, women and children left in Helena. All the men have gone to war."

In our immediate family we had quite a turn out.

James E. Callaway, III, volunteered for the Army and was in the invasion of Africa. He spent the rest of the war in Italy. He was my brother Jim's oldest son. Jim's other son, George, had a hearing disability. Harper L. Jones joined the Navy and spent all the war in training. Harper's brother, L. L. Jones, went into the Army in 1945, when he was old enough. Dr. Gordon L. Doering entered the Army as a Captain and was later promoted to Major in the Dental Corps. He spent his entire service in the Pacific Theater. S. D.

Goza, Jr. went in the Navy as a Lt. J. G. (he had also been in the service in WWI). Lew L. Callaway, Jr. was a Lt., S.G. U.S.N.R. (desk job, N.Y.C.). My children, Peter A. Callaway and Elizabeth Woodson Callaway, were very young.

MEANINGFUL WORK AND THE LATER YEARS

By the time the U.S. entered the war, my father's law practice had returned to being profitable. I was told about one case which he won in 1943. He was then 75 years old. He was on his feet almost constantly for five days during the duration of the trial, which was before a judge and jury. At the conclusion of the trial— when the jury brought in their verdict for my father— everyone in the courtroom gave him a standing ovation, including the Judge, the jury and the opposing attorneys.

He had planned to retire at the end of the war. He and his wife were living alone. His children were all grown and self-supporting and happily married. He began writing again. Some of his historical material went to the new *Montana The Magazine of Western History*. In the Spring 1943 he had written "Something About the Territorial Judges" for Volume 4 of the *Montana Law Review*. He followed this the next spring with "Justices of the Supreme Court of Montana" in Volume 5 of the same publication.

Now he gave more and more of his time to Masonry. In October, 1933, he had been named Inspector General, Honorary 33rd degree. The Judge had earned this honor through 42 years of work in Masonry.

My father died of a heart attack, August 6, 1951, in his home, Helena, Montana. "Throughout his service as a jurist, his opinions were consistently built upon a very careful statement of the facts. Indeed, his outstanding characteristic as a Judge was found in his search for, and obedience to the facts of record." These words are part of the tribute to my father prepared by his fellow jurists and lawyers in the "In Memoriam" presented to the Supreme Court of Montana.

The funeral services were in the hands of his beloved Masonic fraternity. His body rested in the main hall of the Consistory Shrine Temple, and Masons from every Masonic chapter in the state—hundreds and hundreds of men and women—came to pay their final respects to the leader of the Montana fraternity and to the jurist who had held the highest elective office in the state judiciary.

The funeral cortege, which accompanied the casket to Forestvale Cemetery after the Masonic services in the Temple, stretched for miles. It was one of the largest funeral gatherings ever witnessed in Helena. While the funeral procession rolled through Helena, the old fire tower alarm bell tolled constantly. Now located in front of the Civic Center, the bell had originally been situated on a high hill near Last Chance Gulch. It was to alert people in case of fire, and Lew Callaway had played around it as a small boy.

Judge Callaway's obituary in the *New York Times* was an impressive three column, seven inch-deep story accompanied by a picture of the Judge—quite an honor for a Montana man. The Montana papers were lavish in their praise of Judge Lew L. Callaway, who always dispensed "justice regardless of technicalities."

NELL CALLAWAY: BELOVED SURVIVOR

It was decided that my mother should accompany me back to my home in Westport, Connecticut, for a month's rest. Here she could have a quiet time with my wife Helene and our children, Peter and Betsy. Fortunately, the weather in Westport was lovely, and my mother could sit outdoors on the back porch, looking down on the river that ran below our property, and begin the task of answering the hundreds of letters of condolence.

Financially, my mother was in a pretty tight situation. Despite all the years the Judge had worked for the State and the Counties, he had no pension of any kind. My father did leave a relatively small amount of life insurance and, fortunately, the family house was clear of all debt, having been purchased for cash in 1922.

Ellen Badger Callaway, "Nell," was a wonderfully strong and good-looking woman, who was quite determined to run her household by herself. She never complained and never asked for sympathy. She had a beautiful disposition and was a fine manager; she could really stretch a dollar. I helped with a monthly check.

My oldest sister Miriam, "Mimi," continued to live with Nell, doing more than her share to keep the household running, until she remarried. Then she moved to a home just across the street, so she almost never left home. My youngest sister Mary Elizabeth, Mrs. Gordon L. Doering, lived at 704 Stuart in an elegant colonial brick house with her husband and their three sons and two daughters. All of the children loved their grandmother Nellie, so she was always in good company.

My mother's health remained very good indeed. Every fall I arranged for my mother and sister Mimi to spend a month in Westport. They were able to see the best shows on Broadway and many good musical comedies, which they loved. They also enjoyed the hospitality of Mrs. John Chapman, my wife's sister, in her beautiful old 1720 Westport house. She was married to the well-known theatre critic John Chapman, who helped us get tickets to the best shows.

I also made it a point to stop in Helena whenever I travelled to the Pacific coast for *Fortune* or *Sports Illustrated*, and later when I was publisher of

Newsweek, in order to see my mother and sisters. My mother was a spirited woman, always cheerful, popular with men and women alike, and especially popular with all of her nine grandchildren, whom she loved. Living as she did, in her own home, surrounded by the many who loved her in the city she knew so well, she led a happy and fulfilling life.

Nell became somewhat frail in her 89th year, but had constant and loving care from her two daughters, Mimi and Mary. Finally, the end came on her 90th birthday, August 31, 1966. Her children were all there, as well as many grandchildren. After memorial services in the Episcopal church, she was laid to rest beside her husband in the family plot in Forestvale cemetery. She had lived a most remarkable life, was always a tremendous help to her husband, a great and loving mother to her children and grandchildren. Her doctor for many, many years, Thomas Hawkins, wrote me the following words of praise: "In my many years of medical practice, Nell Callaway was the only woman that I could truly say was a saint."

EPILOGUE

The following pages contain an appreciation of some of Judge Callaway's legal decisions on water rights and mining cases by the Honorable Robert Edwin Sullivan, lawyer and educator.

Mr. Sullivan was Dean of the Law School, University of Montana at Missoula, for 23 years. He is a graduate of the University of Notre Dame, A.B. 1940. He was a Major in the U.S.A. Air Force from 1942–45, Earned a J.D. from Notre Dame in 1946, and an L.L.D. from Carroll College in 1965. From 1947–54, he was a Professor of Law at the University of Notre Dame.

In 1979, he was named Vice President and General Counsel of the Montana Power Company and served in this important position until 1983. He is author of *Handbook of Oil & Gas Law 1955* and *Conservation of Oil & Gas: A Legal History 1948–58.*

19

AN APPRECIATION

LLEWELLYN LINK CALLAWAY
CHIEF JUSTICE
MONTANA SUPREME COURT
1922–1934

BY ROBERT E. SULLIVAN

> Chief Justice Callaway's opinions were consistently built upon a very careful statement of the facts. Indeed, his outstanding characteristic as a Judge was found in his search for, and obedience to the facts of record. It is true that he was wont to spend much time and effort in looking carefully into minute details which might, conceivably, have a bearing upon the case before him and that he insisted on having it made clear what their effect might be, or that, rationally, they were without effect; he constantly strove to present the facts in their sequential relation. A departure from the record, an inference "without parentage in the facts", were to him equally abhorrent. Beyond question, his patient attention to detail and his insistence on the dominance of the facts exposed by the record gave his opinions an order and force that leaves the reader with the assurance that the facts had been faced, recognized for what they were, and the law laid, accordingly, upon a solid foundation. Since his opinions were responsive to the facts they were contemporary with their occurrence,—abreast of the times.

This accolade is a part of the *Resolution of Tribute* presented to the Montana Supreme Court by a committee appointed by the Court. The committee was comprised of lawyers and judges who knew Chief Justice Callaway, were familiar with his opinions, and had observed his demeanor and administration of the Court. It included his good friend, partner in the practice of law, and colleague on the bench, the Honorable Charles N. Pray, who had been appointed United States District Judge for Montana by President Calvin Coolidge and continued to serve until his successor was appointed by President Eisenhower.

The opinions of the Callaway Court comprise thirty-three volumes, 65 through 97, of the *Montana Reports*. They include over fifty water law cases. Chief Justice Callaway wrote eighteen of them. He brought to the Court an extensive background, and was recognized as a specialist, in water rights litigation. His opinions as Chief Justice demonstrate meticulous attention to detail and a perspective gleaned from the history and uniqueness of water as one of the most valuable natural resources of the West. Basic legal concepts were restated in succinct language. Interspersed with the analysis and evaluation of the matter before the Court are vignettes of Montana history, admonitions to lawyers in the case, and "one liners"—humorous references to a factual element in the case. Although these asides are not numerous, they blend into the context of the opinion and provide insight into qualities of the Chief Justice which transcend the dignity of the Court.

A determination of the facts is a prerequisite to the resolution of a dispute. To Chief Justice Callaway, facts were things as they are, not as a person would like or perceive them to be. On occasion, some of the facts were difficult to ascertain:

> In water suits in which members of this court have been engaged the trial judges have been confronted with aged witnesses who testified to what took place in early days. These venerable men, having more or less knowledge of what they testified about, frequently looked through mental magnifying-glasses in attempting to recall forgotten things from bygone days. The difficulty encountered in attempting to do equal and exact justice upon testimony of this character is always great and sometimes insuperable.
>
> . . .
>
> The trial court was confronted with that condition which frequently appears in water suits where old rights are involved: All or nearly all of the settlers who did the original work are gone. Those who do appear are hampered with failing memories or are unable to dissociate fact from hearsay. Neighbors testify from impressions remaining after the lapse of years; much of their testimony is guesswork. Men who were boys when the things inquired about were being done appear, and their testimony is colored by the free

> fancies of boyhood which memory still retains. So the appellate as well as the trial court must do the best it can with what it has to work with.
>
> . . .
>
> The record is very imperfect. In fact, if we had been inclined to be technical, we might well have refused to consider it. Nevertheless, we have examined it patiently. After its careful consideration, aided by the briefs of counsel, we are satisfied that error has not been shown.
>
> . . .
>
> After a further study of the record together with the supplemental briefs we are unable to reach conclusions which are satisfactory to us; but, as the parties seem to have produced all the evidence within their command no good purpose would be served by sending back the case, or any part of it, for a new trial.

In the American legal system, lawyers are officers of the Court. Without impairing in any way the duty to represent their clients, lawyers as counsel of record in a case have the obligation to assist the Court. On occasion, a lawyer would fail to accept the duty to the Court imposed by this relationship. As the Resolution of Tribute stated:

> There was no doubt in the minds of his colleagues or of members of the bar as to who was the Chief Justice. In conference, he labored to produce a unanimity of view, without deserting principle, but he did not hesitate to dissent if he regarded the views of the majority without firm support in the record, or as disregarding legal principles applicable to the facts.

To borrow an expression of the day, "he ran a tight ship":

> The pleader would have saved himself, and others later concerned, much labor if he had stated his facts in ordinary and concise language. The complaint before us is awkward in construction, carrying a

suspicion, at least, that the pleader's theory of plaintiff's legal rights is not clear.

. . .

Plaintiff's counsel denounce defendant's conduct throughout the entire transaction in language plain and forcible. Whether or not their castigation of defendant is justified, it is manifest that vigorous language now does not excuse plaintiff's passivity during the long lapse of time following the date when he accepted, over his protest as he says, the deed executed to him.

. . .

The plaintiff failed to establish any right in the ditch by contract; on this feature of the case there was an utter failure of proof. In this situation he sought to save himself by proving that he had acquired title by adverse use. Whether the pleadings warranted the reception of evidence upon this theory we need not determine. We shall decide the case upon the evidence admitted.

. . .

The record in this case is voluminous. The transcript, in three volumes, embraces 910 pages, and the exhibits embrace many more. The transcript contains much useless matter. The stenographer seems to have caught every word said. So we find in the record discussions about taking recesses, numerous jokes of counsel and idle talk with witnesses—"visiting," the court called it in reproving counsel. A page and a half of the transcript is taken up with an investigation as to how a witness came by the title of "Major." None of this useless matter should have been permitted in the bill of exceptions. We recommend that trial judges refuse to certify bills of exception containing matter which clearly has nothing to do with the merits of the case. For this transgression of Supreme Court Rule XVII the defendant shall pay one-third the cost of the transcript. Otherwise the defendant shall be entitled to its costs upon this appeal.

The Callaway opinions are more than the resolution of water right disputes. Several of them provide vignettes of Montana history:

> The rationale of the [1877] Act is plain when we consider the history of the period which gave rise to the necessity for its enactment. Placer mining was still in vigorous operation in all the principal "gulches" and in many of the lesser ones. It was impossible advantageously to move the auriferous gravels from their beds without the use of powerful heads of water. Most of the gulch channels did not produce a sufficient amount. The necessity for large bodies of water increased as the gravels became less productive. It was the practice from the earliest days to bring in bodies of water from adjacent streams for use in mining. Some of the necessary ditches and flumes were long and expensive. Companies were organized for the purpose of supplying water which they sold to placer miners at a certain rate per miner's inch. As an illustration, the first legislative assembly created James H. Febes and another, their associates or assigns, a body corporate by the name of the Rams Horn Ditch Company, authorizing the company to take water from Rams Horn Creek, and to convey it to Bevins Gulch, and thence to other mining districts "as said water can be led and used to advantage." The company was authorized "to sell water to purchasers at the following rates: for the first use of water fifty cents per inch and all other uses not to exceed twenty-five cents per inch per day."
>
> . . .
>
> When active mining closed in the gulch the evidence does not show, nor does it show what became of the mining ground and water rights. If the facts were disclosed, probably they would tell the familiar story of the early-day placer miner—when his claim "played out," undauntedly and hopefully he set out for other and still richer diggings, regardless of the old.
>
> . . .

In Montana, as elsewhere, when the early settlers made their original appropriations they had little knowledge of the quantity of water necessary to irrigate their lands to good advantage. Ample quantities of water being available in the streams the settlers claimed extravagant amounts. While usually the ditches were comparatively small at first, these grew in size from year to year. To a large extent this was necessary as the settlers increased their cultivated areas as their means permitted. But the duty of water was seldom, if ever, understood. Almost every irrigator used an excessive amount of water, some all they could get. Some actually washed the seed out of the ground. In the irrigation of hay and pasture lands it was a common practice to "irrigate on horseback," that is, the irrigator went on horseback with his shovel to his main ditch or laterals at intervals—and sometimes at long intervals—and "changed his water." The statutes of 1907 and 1921 relating to the appropriation of water from adjudicated streams were designed to compel those who sought to appropriate water from such streams to become bound, as are parties and privies thereto, by all of the provisions of the decree or decrees by which the rights of the parties thereto had been determined. Experience had shown that after the rights of all of the parties taking water from a stream had been adjudicated, a subsequent appropriator would appear upon the scene, tap the stream and ruthlessly take the water, disregarding the decreed rights and flaunting the orders of the commissioner appointed by the court to distribute the water according to the terms of the decree. The only remedy the prior appropriators had was to commence a suit against the new appropriator, the result being that all of the rights of the stream had again to be adjudicated; and after that decree was entered if another subsequent appropriator took the water the same process had to be gone over again. Unquestionably the legislature of 1921 intended that an appropriation of the waters of an adjudicated stream should not be made thereafter without a substantial compliance with the requirements of the statute then enacted.

These vignettes of Montana history were not confined to extracts from his opinions as Chief Justice. He reminisced in 1943, in Volume 4 of the *Montana Law Review*, about Montana Territorial Court Judges:

> My memory of the first jurists of Montana is pretty dim, naturally. That I should have known some of them early, in the circumstances, is easy to understand. My father took the position of Secretary of Montana in the latter part of March, 1871. The Secretary of a Territory is of considerable importance; he is in fact Lieutenant Governor, Secretary of State, Comptroller, and has other duties. He acts as Governor when that officer is absent which is not infrequent. Of course he becomes acquainted with the "official family" at once and shortly knows about everyone in the Territory that's worth knowing, and a good many that are not.
>
> The Secretary and his lady had prominent people at their house often; Virginia, the Capital, was the "social city." Among these was Hezekiah L. Hosmer, first Chief Justice, the man who opened the first district court in Montana, and who in 1871 was Postmaster of the city. My memory of him is not clear, but he played with me.
>
> At the beginning the Chief Justice was in a difficult place. He was the presiding Judge in the city in which the Vigilante organization was founded, and in which that organization existed for a considerable time, even after the Chief Justice had arrived. The people, or some of them, viewed courts with distrust. The administration of the Vigilantes, fierce at times, was just and it certainly was efficacious. In its action there was little delay; from its judgements no appeal.
>
> Judge Hosmer was a wise man. That he appreciated the local condition is shown by his charge to the first Grand Jury December 5, 1864. A citizen who had listened to the charge remarked to the Judge: "We are glad the government has sent you here. We have some

civil matters to attend to, but you had better let us take charge of criminal affairs."

As trial Judge [Thomas C. Bach], as were all members of the Court in Territorial days, he was punctilious in his government of the Court. The Bailiffs had to keep everything just so. At Fort Benton in early September, he opened court and summoned a jury from the county. Men came in from the ranches and herds, of course. The Judge, not to be too severe on the day the jurors came in, asked them the necessary questions and swore them as members of the jury panel. But, the story goes, it was different next day. Upon taking the Bench he delivered a homily on the deportment and duties of a juror, then called the first case and directed the Clerk to call a jury. As they filed into a box a juror appeared without a coat. The Judge said, "Mr. Juror, don't you know it is not proper to appear in court without a coat? Have you no coat?" "Yes sir." "Where is it?" "At home." "Get it." The juror left the court room in a hurry. The Judge said, "Mr. Sheriff, adjourn this court for ten minutes." But the juror hadn't returned in ten minutes, nor did he return during the next half hour. The Judge said, "Mr. Sheriff, where did that juror go?" The sheriff replied, with a twinkle in his eye, "The last I saw of him he was on his horse, said he was going home for his coat." "Where does he live?" "About 40 miles from town," the sheriff said.

The judges who served the Territory were Presidential appointees. Most of them started in with the handicap of being designated "carpet baggers." The people thought the Judges came to serve out their terms only, expecting them to leave the Territory when the salary ceased; and many did so. The people looked askance upon these judges, and mildly resented the rule of those whom they regarded as mere temporary federal employees. Nevertheless, the Montanans were courteous and friendly to the distinguished gentlemen.

The judges came into an unsettled region, sparsely settled, the towns far apart, travel between arduous, mostly by stage coach. For example, at first one could go by stage from Virginia City to Helena, the most populous towns, in less than 24 hours. As business slowed, it took a day and a night, and eventually, the journey settled down to two days, stopping overnight at Whitehall. This is indication of travel over the Territory. In the flush days one had to keep his seat in the stage coach or he would lose it.

Accommodations for holding court were few. It will be remembered that Judge Hosmer held his first court in the dining room of the Planter's Hotel in Virginia City, one table being placed upon another to give him elevation, the upper table serving as the "bench." Gradually, better accommodations were provided. A court room properly equipped had two jury panels, one for the grand jury and one for the petit. The chairs were rigid affairs. There were no swivel chairs enabling the juror to squirm around or lean backward to assuage his feelings in the long day. I claim to have been the first district judge to put pliable swivel chairs into a court room in Montana.

The Territorial judges were confronted with a great variety of litigation and few law books were available. The law of mining and water rights was in a formative state. Montana has not followed California consistently either in mining or water right law; on the contrary, our courts have struck out boldly declaring principles which have seemed to them best suited to our conditions, conformable to our own policies and statutes.

The Bannock statutes were taken mostly from California. Generally speaking, we followed the California decisions in our earlier days. If a lawyer cited a California case in point he won his law suit, so every lawyer of any prominence had in his office the Montana and California Reports. Many had little else. In the 80's it became the fashion to buy law books, and many fine individual law libraries were to be found in Montana. Upon the advent of the State it began to

> build up a State law library, now one of the best in the country. The members of the new Supreme Court were students making use of law books. These alone do not make a good lawyer or a good judge. One must have a lawyerlike mind and cultivate it; a good lawyer must be a clear thinker. This was the view of the renowned lawyer and orator, Wilbur F. Sanders, a dominant figure in Territorial life and in early statehood. The Colonel was a scholar and student, but he did not believe in following a dictum simply because someone, or some court, said it. Seeing Mr. Clayberg receiving some large boxes he inquired, "What have you in those boxes?" To which Clayberg replied "Books!" with an inflection that irritated the Colonel, who then asked "What kind of books?" "Law books, damn ye," said Clayberg. "Hum," said the Colonel, "law books confuse the mind."
>
> After 1880 I knew something of the general reputation of all the Territorial Judges. So far as I know there wasn't an unworthy Judge among them. The Territory was fortunate that it was served by such a patriotic, honorable and able body of men.

If Chief Justice Callaway had judges as role models, among them could have been William T. Pigott, first elected to the Montana Supreme Court in 1898, and Chief Justice Theodore Brantly, whom Callaway replaced as Chief Justice in 1922. His reminiscences of the Justices of the Montana Supreme Court are found in Volume 5 of the *Montana Law Review*:

> Judge Pigott displayed unusual strength as a lawyer. He reveled in abstract propositions. His mind was so logical that it naturally had a trend to the exact which brought down the criticism that he was inclined to be technical. He was, however, broad-minded; his disposition was to arrive at justice. There was nothing small about him. He was a prodigious worker, anxious to arrive at a correct decision without the slightest regard for personalities, the rich man or the poor man. Private citizen and powerful corporation stood alike

before his eyes. So solicitous of arriving at a correct decision was he that often he lay awake at night, turning and turning in his bed, thinking over some intricate legal problem.

[Judge Brantly] was universally regarded as one of the ablest district judges in the State. This eminence caused his nomination and subsequent election as Chief Justice of the Supreme Court. He took his seat on January 3, 1899. He was re-elected in 1904, 1910, and 1916; thus he served as Chief Justice nearly a quarter of a century. His judicial service covered the most momentous period in this state's history. His work as district judge had been arduous and difficult, but he frequently said that the most laborious and exhausting period of his life was the first four years of his service as Chief Justice. This was "because of the multitude of perplexing and troublesome issues and problems then existing" in Montana. That period was known to history as the "copper war." A multitude of other difficult questions arose for solution during the first decade of the new century. Judge Brantly possessed a strong sense of justice, great industry, and large ability. His integrity was unquestioned, his determination to reach a right result remarkable. A sound lawyer, committed to the theory that a judge should declare the law as it exists, and not as he might fancy it might better be, his mind was not fettered with outworn rules supposed to have been apposite to an earlier period, the exigency which brought them into being having long since passed; he sought the substance rather than the shadow. So when the time came in our judicial history that wrong defeated justice because under the devise of ancient remedies the law seemed without remedy, in harmony with the maxim that "for every wrong there is a remedy," the Chief Justice declared the Constitution of Montana warrants the issuance of a writ of supervisory control. The impact of this decision upon litigation was, and has continued to be, tremendous in this state. Used within proper limitations this extraordinary writ has been a great step forward in the administration of justice.

The Callaway opinions reflect an understanding of the value and the propensities of water, the difficulty of orderly allocation among several claimants, and the purpose of legislation that addressed particular problems:

> Montana has many millions of arid, irrigable lands. With irrigation these, instead of arid would be teeming acres. Experience has shown that lands of this character, now mere grazing lands, with irrigation prove productive to a high degree. Montana also discharges across its borders flood and surplus waters more than sufficient annually to cover its irrigable lands. When this water is impounded and conserved these vast areas, now fit only for ranging livestock, will ascend to the higher adaptability of supporting contented homes. Every acre of land in this state susceptible to irrigation should be cultivated. Between irrigating seasons the water of Montana's numerous streams mostly goes to waste, and generally speaking, in high-water time, which usually is in June, tremendous quantities of flood waters run away without serving any useful purpose. The construction and maintenance of secure reservoirs for the conservation of these waters, therefore, is of very high public importance.
>
> . . .
>
> It is to the interest of the public that water be conserved for use rather than be permitted to go to waste, to the end that the arid lands of the state may be put under irrigation and thus be made productive.
>
> . . .
>
> The use of water in Montana is vital to the prosperity of our people. Its use, even by an individual, to irrigate a farm, is so much a contributing factor to the welfare of the state that the people in adopting the Constitution declared it to be a public use.
>
> . . .
>
> It is a matter of common knowledge in the several judicial districts of this state where irrigation has been

> practiced since the early days that extravagant quantities of water were awarded the litigants by the courts. In instances more water was awarded than some of the ditches of the litigants ever would carry; in others much greater quantities of water than the litigants ever did or could use beneficially. In some cases the courts were not to blame. The litigants agreed to get all they could. They even stipulated to the use of quantities of water ridiculously large for the amount of land irrigated.
>
> . . .
>
> The rule contended for by plaintiff would lead us into "a morass of practical difficulties and doctrinal refinements." It would disturb the settled policy upon which the owners of water rights of this state have depended, founded upon the decisions of this court, through the long course of the years. Derangement of a policy so deeply rooted is not to be contemplated except under a compelling necessity, which does not seem to exist.
>
> . . .
>
> The purpose of the law-making body in enacting the statutes relating to the appropriation of water in an adjudicated stream was to avoid useless water suits (again involving the entire subject matter), to provide security for those whose water rights already have been adjudicated, to compel those who seek the establishment of a water right in an adjudicated stream to take that water right subject to rights already fixed and determined, after bona fide litigation, by the decree of a competent court.

The writing style of the Callaway opinions was distinctive. The Resolution of Tribute described the components:

> None of his opinions were freighted with verbiage; they exhibited a decided preference for pithy speech, the terse, stout Anglo-Saxon words that penetrate the mind. Not infrequently his opinions reveal an epigrammatic flavor; sometimes his expressions were

> folksy and homespun. There was no diplomacy in them, but there was sincerity.

Justice Cardozo of the United States Supreme Court cautioned that words are sharp instruments; if they are not handled carefully, they may cut your fingers. Chief Justice Callaway used language carefully, deliberately, and effectively. His opinions are legal literature of the highest order. They are fine examples of the art of communication, not merely the finality of a decision.

> It is elementary that the appropriator of the water of a running stream does not own the corpus of the water; he owns only the right to use it. If the water in a running stream is unclaimed and unappropriated, it would be an absurdity to say that anyone owns the right to use it.
>
> . . .
>
> One should not be permitted to play the dog in the manger with water he does not or cannot use for a beneficial purpose when other lands are crying for water. It is to the interest of the public that every acre of land in this state susceptible to irrigation shall be irrigated. It is the writer's opinion that the legislature should enact a statute to the effect that, where one has not made a beneficial use of the whole or some part of the water claimed by or decreed to him, for a specified number of years, the part so unused shall be deemed abandoned.
>
> . . .
>
> He is simply a junior appropriator, with the rights and the disabilities of one who may use water from a stream subject to the superior rights of others.
>
> . . .
>
> Because of the nature of the right [to water by adverse user], the elements constituting it must be proven satisfactorily and unequivocally; and no doubtful inference will suffice. The right by adverse user, or

> prescription, is acquired, in some measure, by an invasion of the rights of others—it bears a sort of kinship, by refined descent, to the "possession by bow and spear" of an earlier time; it is based upon a positive assertion of right in and by the water user in derogation of the rights of everyone else.
>
> . . .
>
> Notwithstanding the effect of *res judicata* to litigation in general, it is not like unto the laws of the Medes and Persians.
>
> . . .
>
> He thus would take from her that which not enriches him but makes her poor indeed, to paraphrase Iago's celebrated saying. (Shak. Othello, act III, scene III).
>
> . . .
>
> It is an odd conceit that a court by procedural directions to one litigant may fix the characteristic of the unrelated property rights of another.
>
> . . .
>
> Perfection in the taxation of property is not attainable, nor is it expected. It is expected and required of the taxing authorities that all property shall be taxed at its full cash value as near as may be, the fallibility of human judgment considered.

"His search for, and obedience to the facts of record" has been discussed previously. This was accompanied by a synthesis of the history of land and water use in Montana and of the abstract legal concept of ownership, not of water itself, but of a right to use the water for a beneficial purpose. The Callaway opinions reflect a clarity of thought, preciseness of expression, and use of readily understandable language. In several cases they are cogent restatements of fundamental principles of water law:

> The quantity of water which may be claimed lawfully under a prior appropriation is limited to that quantity

within the amount claimed which the appropriator has needed, and which within a reasonable time he has actually and economically applied to a beneficial use.

. . .

When there was sufficient water in the creeks to supply the actual needs of prior appropriators there could be no such thing as adverse use. Each party to the decree is entitled to the use of the water and it is only when it becomes so scarce that all of the parties cannot be supplied that an appropriator by taking that which by priority belongs to another can be said to initiate an adverse use.

. . .

"Excess" or "surplus" water, as these words are used by water-right lawyers, mean simply water which is flowing in the stream in addition to what may be termed adjudicated waters.

. . .

Water used in irrigation, except that which escapes control and runs away upon the surface, sinks in the ground; and, less that part which is consumed by plant life "mingles with the soil and remains suspended therein," or by percolation reaches bedrock, which frequently is the bed of a stream. Becoming part of the stream, it is available for further use, and subject to appropriation. It is by "this process of returning to the stream after use that makes it possible for the same volume of water, or a major part of it, to supply many persons, . . . even though the first appropriator claims the whole volume, and can, at times, or even constantly, use the same for some industrial purpose, because such use does not usually swallow it, but leaves it available to others. But by such an appropriation the first appropriator does not acquire a pre-emption of the whole creek, so that he, or his successor, may, after enjoying the use of it for some beneficial purpose, convey the creek away and cut off subsequent appropriators. Therefore a subse-

> quent right to use the same water, or so much of it as returns to the creek, and to use the waters of the creek when the first is not using the same, may be acquired."
>
> Such, we are convinced, are settled principles with respect to waste and percolating waters.
>
> . . .
>
> Without reference to the right of a land owner to control underground water upon his own land, when it joins a natural stream it becomes a part of that stream and is *publici juris*. This comes down by gradations from the civil law doctrine of "the negative community."
>
> . . .
>
> The owner of land with an appurtenant water right may, by appropriate conveyance, convey the land to one person and the water right to another. But, if he conveys the land without reservation, he also conveys the appurtenance and whatever is incidental to the land. He therefore conveys the appurtenant water rights, unless he expressly reserves them.
>
> . . .
>
> Where the water right intended to be conveyed with the land is stated in express terms, the grantee takes that only which is expressly conveyed. He does not take any additional rights by implication. In such case the grantor reserves what he does not convey.

But there was also a humorous strain in the Chief Justice. Those who knew him discerned it readily. Those who read the Callaway opinions must be sensitive to it to recognize it. *The Resolution of Tribute* described it:

> He could smile easily, or chuckle heartily, if penetrating wit or happy circumstance permitted during argument—indeed, he might, very quietly, provide either; on the other hand, he brooked no interference with orderly procedures, and would not tolerate any breach

of decorum on the part of members of the Bar, or spectators in the Courtroom.

His opinions contain examples of it:

> We are constrained to believe that the provision in the decree, above quoted, rather than tending to clarify the situation, tends to confuse it—it muddies the water.
>
> . . .
>
> It is interesting to note here that there was filed for record August 11, 1883 at 8:00 o'clock a.m. (the county clerks got up early in those days) a notice of appropriation.

Among the water rights opinions by Chief Justice Callaway, the one in Rock Creek Ditch and Flume Co. v. Miller is of special interest. The facts were unique and the case has been cited extensively as a precedent, not only by Montana courts but by courts of other states. This was not uncommon. Other opinions of the Callaway Court and by the Chief Justice continue to be cited with approval as precedent.

In the Rock Creek case, plaintiff company brought water for irrigation from one watershed over a ridge to a separate watershed, by a canal seven miles long, for sale to its stockholders. Three years earlier, defendant had appropriated water from a natural stream in this second watershed for irrigation. A spring was the primary source of water for the stream. Subsequent irrigation by one of the stockholders from the canal increased the flow of water from the spring substantially. However, the canal ended a mile from the spring and there was no surface channel connecting the canal and the spring. The increased flow was from underground seepage. Several years later another stockholder constructed a dam and a ditch leading from the spring to take water for irrigation. Defendant tore out the dam. This lawsuit followed.

J. E. Corette, then practicing law in Missoula, argued the case for the plaintiff. It was his first case before the Montana Supreme Court. Almost sixty years later, his recollection is still a vivid one:

> Chief Justice Callaway stated Plaintiff theory as follows:
>
> "It is the contention of the plaintiff that it at all times has been entitled to the use for sale to its customers and stockholders of all the water brought into the basin and that the same has never been the proper subject of appropriation by the defendants, since it has never constituted a part of the natural flow of any stream."
>
> Chief Justice Callaway then went back through the history of both civil and common law jurisprudence starting with the Institutes of Justinian: ["By natural law these things are common to all, viz.: air, running water, the sea, and as a consequence the shores of the sea."] and the civil law doctrine written by the learned French jurist Pothier: ["The first of mankind had in common all those things which God had given to the human race. This community was not a positive community of interest, like that which exists between several persons who have the ownership of a thing in which each has his particular portion. It is a community which those who have written on this subject have called a negative community, which resulted from the fact that those things which were common to all belonged no more to one than to the others."]
>
> He then discussed some of the decisions in other states of the United States and all of the decisions of the Montana Supreme Court to support his opinion that (1) an appropriator does not own and cannot acquire the corpus of the water, but only the right to use it even though the water was not part of the natural flow in the new watershed and had been imported; (2) that imported water is not developed water; and (3) that water once used which by return

> flow reached the stream bed or spring can be appropriated and cannot be reclaimed by the original user other than through appropriation of that water.
>
> It was a very difficult decision because the equities strongly favored the Plaintiffs who were young immigrants from Europe and who had made the imported water available in the area at extraordinary expense and effort and the defendant had done nothing but appropriate the water from the spring and stream bed and use it.
>
> Chief Justice Callaway, with his characteristic thoroughness and thoughtfulness, also examined all of the Montana decisions on developed water, ground water, and return flow that had been recaptured, and water gathered, collected, used and sold by the early day gold placer miners to support his conclusion that one can acquire only the right to use and not the corpus of the water. The decision was unanimous.
>
> This scholarly opinion of Justice Callaway settled basic questions not previously decided regarding the ownership, as distinguished from the right to use of water that had been appropriated in one watershed and been transported over the dividing hills to another watershed for beneficial use and sale in that watershed.

The recognition of Chief Justice Callaway as an outstanding jurist was not limited to the State of Montana or to the West. John H. Wigmore, distinguished legal scholar, author of the treatise on the *Law of Evidence*, and described as "a champion of sound legal reforms," wrote in a letter dated July 26, 1934, as follows:

> As you may know, it is a part of my duty to examine carefully, for the purpose of keeping up with my subject of Evidence, all the opinions of Supreme State Courts. During this last year I have completed a survey of the Supreme Court decisions in all the States

> for the last ten years. In my opinion Judge Callaway is one of the best jurists now on any Supreme Bench. Not only are his opinions clear and rational, but they exhibit a liberality of view, and a readiness to keep up with the modern growth of law. These are days when the community looks to the Courts to decide cases, not only in accordance with fundamental principles, but also in the light of changing conditions that lead to new cases and new combinations of fact. The Courts, without departing from the fundamentals, can in this process adapt those fundamentals to the new conditions and new problems. Judge Callaway is notably among those Judges who exemplify this ideal. There are Judges who do not appreciate the situation, but Judge Callaway is the last one in the world of whom this reproach could be uttered. He had emphatically kept modern opinions in step with modern times.

As law, the opinions of the Callaway Court and those written by the Chief Justice continue to be important. Albert Stone, Professor at the University of Montana Law School and recognized nationally as a scholar of water law, observes in the preface to his prognosis *Montana Water Law for the 1980's*:

> Nearly all water rights were acquired pursuant to statutory and case law as it existed prior to 1973, and it is those rights that are going to be determined in future lawsuits and major adjudications. To know what those rights are, one absolutely *must* know what the law was at the time those rights were acquired.

Although the Callaway Court was not mentioned specifically in that context, Professor Stone has written elsewhere:

> Clearly this period, 1922 to 1934 when Llewellyn L. Callaway was Chief Justice of the Montana Supreme Court, was a very active as well as a developmental period for Montana water law. . . .The cases from this era, this Court, and particularly Chief Justice Callaway have greatly contributed to Montana water law as it exists today.

Honorable W. W. Lessley, first Judge of the Montana Water Court, in a 1988 decision wrote:

> We approach this crucial question with the words of Justice Llewellyn Callaway (coming down from our early history); Callaway was one of the stalwarts in this troublesome field of law. [Then quoting from a 1909 opinion by District Judge Callaway, participating in the Supreme Court case in the place of one of the Justices and writing the opinion.]

Honorable C. Bruce Loble, Chief Judge of the Montana Water Court, summarized the influence of the Chief Justice on water law to the present day:

> It is the opinions of Chief Justice Callaway and others that guide the Montana Water Court in its mission to adjudicate the waters of Montana. This Court has relied on the opinions of Chief Justice Callaway on many occasions in the Court's search for what the law was at the time early water rights were first acquired. The Court does so because, as pointed out in the Resolution of Tribute, Chief Justice Callaway's opinions were built upon a careful statement of the facts. The care in which he crafted his opinions is very important to the Montana Water Court. Although the specifics of factual situations in water right disputes can vary, there is still substantial modern similarities to the ancient cases. Disputes over water have not changed much since the Philistines and the Herdsmen of Gerar "strove" with Isaac and cried out the "water is ours" (Genesis 26:12-33). We hear the same cry today.
>
> Unfortunately, one of the consistent threads in human conflict is that over the allocation of water. Chief Justice Callaway's careful recitation of facts is extremely important in arriving at a consistent and fair application of the ancient water law. His involvement in water law began long before his ascension to the Montana Supreme Court. As a lawyer, a district judge and finally as Chief Justice, the influence of Llewellyn Callaway on Montana water law will reach far into the

twenty-first century.

Opinions of the Callaway Court and those of the Chief Justice continue to be quoted and cited in law journals, proceedings of natural resource conferences, treatises on water law, and in proceedings before water law tribunals and courts. Professor Stone has said, "Most of these cases are cited and several are discussed in detail in the Water Law course at the University of Montana Law School." A required reading list inserted in a training manual for newly employed Water Masters in Montana includes several opinions of the Chief Justice. In truth, he has left a living legacy.

The life of Llewellyn Link Callaway—man, lawyer, District Judge, and Chief Justice—exemplifies the classical definition of a profession: the practice of a learned art in the spirit of public service. He was devoted to the law, committed to justice, and unselfish in his service to others and to his beloved state.

This Appreciation of Chief Justice Callaway commenced with an extract from the *Resolution of Tribute* composed by a committee of lawyers and judges, all of whom are now deceased, who knew and appreciated him. It was accepted by the Montana Supreme Court and adopted as a part of the Court's official records. It is appropriate that this Appreciation end with an extract from that *Resolution of Tribute*.

> As members of this Court and as members of this Committee recall the years of association in a common endeavor, the clash of mind with mind in the unending struggle to attain in some measure the ideal of justice under law, there lives in memory this man's devotion and loyalty to a great task, the integrity and sturdy independence with which he wrought. For these are the attributes of the Judge, without which there can be no justice. They are the foundation stones and the weight-bearing members of the Temple of Justice.

ACKNOWLEDGEMENT

To Dean Martin Burke of the University of Montana Law School for extensive research assistance, to J. E. Corette, Honorable C. Bruce Loble, Professor Albert Stone, Michael E. Zimmerman, and special thanks to Lew L. Callaway, Jr., for the invitation to prepare this Appreciation. It has been fun.

ACKNOWLEDGEMENTS

It is with gratitude that I recognize the many people who helped, in large ways and small, to create this book.

The major contributor is Vivian A. Paladin, who edited the manuscripts of my father on which the major parts of the book are based. Vivian was for twelve years editor of *Montana The Magazine of Western History*, published by the Montana Historical Society. Through her professional competence, she made it the best of all regional historical journals.

Author of the final and very important chapter is Robert Edwin Sullivan, distinguished lawyer and retired Dean of the University of Montana Law School. Dean Sullivan, a close personal and professional friend for many years, wrote and edited the concluding appreciation of the Supreme Court decisions of my father, especially as they relate to water rights and mining law cases. Valuable assistance in completing this part of the book was given by Martin Burke, currently Dean of the University of Montana Law School, and Professor Albert A. Stone.

Throughout the project, we called on the indispensable Montana Historical Society and received important help from Bob Clark and Dave Walter of the Library and Lory Morrow and Becca Kohl of the Photograph Archives.

My old friend and associate at *Time* and *Newsweek*, William H. Scherman, helped greatly with wise counsel as did Sidney S. Alderman, Mining Geologist, San Francisco. Special thanks to Marcella S. Moriarty who has helped me on this book from its inception.

This book owes its good looks and easy reading to the typeface Bookman, set by Bonnie Lambert of Desktop Type, and to the excellent printing, binding and distribution arranged for by Rick Newby and his associates of Falcon Press/SkyHouse Publishers.

Finally, a personal note. Whenever they were called upon, members of my family gave assistance, freely offering encouragement, advice and pictures from family collections. These special contributors include my son, Peter A. Callaway, and daughter, Elizabeth W. Callaway; my sister, Mary Callaway Doering; niece, Jean Randolph Turpie; and nephew, Dr. Harper L. Jones.

Thank you all.

L. L. CALLAWAY, JR.

August 1991 Napa, California